WISDOM
FROM WILLIE
JEWELS
FROM JESSIE

Simple Lessons to Help You Live a Long and Fulfilling Life

Willie L. Dixon, Sr., Jessie M. Dixon
Angela L. Dixon, Esq.

WWW.SELFPUBLISHN30DAYS.COM

To Willie L. Dixon Jr.,
our son, who made us very proud.
He was a great husband, father, brother, uncle, nephew,
cousin, co-worker, and friend to many.
He is missed terribly.

Published by *Self Publish -N- 30 Days*

© Copyright 2023 Angela Dixon

All rights reserved worldwide. No part of this book may be reproduced or transmitted in any form or by any means, electronic or mechanical, including photocopying, recording, or by any information storage and retrieval system without written permission from Angela L. Dixon, Esq.

Printed in the United States of America

ISBN: 979-8-39449-222-8

1. 2. 3.

Angela L. Dixon, Esq., *Wisdom from Willie, Jewels from Jessie*

Disclaimer/Warning:

This book is intended for lecture and informative purposes only. This publication is designed to provide competent and reliable information regarding the subject matter covered. The author or publisher is not engaged in rendering legal or professional advice. Laws vary from state to state, and if legal, financial, or other expert assistance is needed, the services of a professional should be sought. The author and publisher disclaim any liability that is incurred from the use or application of the contents of this book.

TABLE OF CONTENTS

A Note from Willie and Jessie vii

Introduction by Angela L. Dixon, Esq. 1

Lesson 1 5
ALWAYS REMEMBER WHERE YOU CAME FROM AS IT WILL KEEP YOU GROUNDED

Lesson 2 31
YOUTH IS FOR LEARNING; YOU DON'T HAVE TO GET EVERYTHING RIGHT, BUT YOU CAN LEARN FROM EVERYTHING YOU DO

Lesson 3 39
MARRIAGE AND PARENTING IS A PROCESS, JUST STAY THE COURSE AND DO THE BEST YOU CAN

Lesson 4 51
IN LIFE, YOU MUST WORK TO LIVE, NOT LIVE TO WORK

Lesson 5 63
YOU MAY NOT HAVE A LOT BUT ALWAYS SAVE SOMETHING. SAVING NOW MAY SAVE YOU LATER

Lesson 6 69
OWNING A HOME SHOULD BE A GOAL. IF YOU DESIRE TO HAVE ONE, YOU MUST PLAN, SAVE AND ACT

Lesson 7 77
TO LIVE A LONG LIFE, GROW YOUR OWN FOOD
AND STAY ACTIVE

Lesson 8 89
NO MATTER THE AGE, IF YOU HAVE THE DESIRE
AND ABILITY TO TRAVEL, THEN GO

Lesson 9 109
YOU MAY NOT BE READY FOR LEADERSHIP, BUT
SOMETIMES IT IS READY FOR YOU

Lesson 10 115
LIFE IS FULL OF CHALLENGES; DON'T BE AFRAID.
HAVE FAITH, TAKE THEM ON, AND OVERCOME THEM

Lesson 11 121
WHEREVER YOU MAY GO OR LIVE, FIND THE JOY
THE CITY HAS TO OFFER

Lesson 12 125
ALWAYS REMEMBER THOSE WHO CAME BEFORE
YOU AND THINK OF THOSE WHO WILL COME
AFTER YOU

Lesson 13 135
DON'T TAKE YOURSELF SO SERIOUSLY; MAKE SURE
TO STOP AND SMELL THE ROSES. JUST HAVE FUN!

Lesson 14 151
GIVE PEOPLE THEIR FLOWERS WHILE THEY CAN
STILL SMELL THEM

Conclusion by Angela L. Dixon, Esq.   173

About the Author   175

A NOTE FROM WILLIE AND JESSIE

We never imagined we would write a book. While we have lived a simple life, it has been a wonderful one, full of rich experiences and lovely people to share it with. It was a joy to remember those good times and tell our story.

Some memories bring happiness, and others, sadness. Through it all, we know God is good and has brought us this far. There is a lot that goes into writing a book, especially remembering what happened many, many decades ago. We think we did pretty well, considering.

We hope this book serves as a source of inspiration and history for generations to come. We would like to thank all of our family and friends who contributed to this effort, especially our daughter Angela who came to us with the idea to write this book a few years ago. She was determined to make this happen for us, and we are thankful for it.

Willie and Jessie Dixon Sr.

INTRODUCTION

By Angela L. Dixon, Esq.

I wrote the title for this book on my phone on May 4th, 2018. I am not exactly sure what prompted it, but it was probably my good friend and law school classmate Tracie Melvin. She had come to visit my parents and me a few years before 2018. She had seen the social media posts about my parents discussing my dad's garden, the funny things they would say, noting their many years of marriage, and reminiscing on their upbringing. After spending time with them, she said that my parents should write a book. Of course, I agreed.

The title came to me in the middle of the night. I woke up and sent it in a text to myself at 3:51 a.m. As you can see by the current year (we are in the year 2023), I did not act on it for some time.

On Thanksgiving in 2020, I visited my parent's home. I was sitting down, talking to Mom and Dad, when I announced:

"I am going to write a book on y'all. Is that something y'all want to do?"

"Yes, if you want to," they responded with mellow smiles.

So, *Wisdom from Willie, Jewels from Jessie,* was born. I added the subtitle, *Simple Lessons to Help You Live a Long and Fulfilling Life,* later and decided to write the book from a lesson viewpoint. I noted some subject areas for the chapters and decided to go out and buy some notebooks and pens to allow mom and dad to get their writing started. I thought if they put their thoughts down in their own words, it would give more ownership to the process.

I wrote down all the topics of interest for the chapters and told them to write their thoughts and what they remembered from their past. I then went to my home in Houston and did not think a lot about it.

When I returned to Alabama for Christmas, Mom brought me their notebooks and told me, "This is what we wrote so far."

As I flipped through the notebooks, I found pages and pages of information. I was shocked! I wasn't sure what I had expected, but clearly, they were ready to tell their stories and ready to be heard. When I saw all they had accomplished in such a short time, I knew I had to get in gear and start working. It was a process, but we made it.

I began writing this introduction while sitting at the beach on Galveston Island, Texas. The date was October 6th, 2021. A few days before, my aunt, Bonnie Richardson, (my dad's older sister and last living sibling) left us to take her place with our ancestors. She was the matriarch of our family, and at ninety-two years old, lived a good, long life. She had so many personal stories to tell me about my grandparents, her siblings and herself from her childhood in Nicholsville, Alabama.

Losing her was heartbreaking, but what made it worse was that I never wrote her stories down. I just listened to them as she told them whenever I would visit. While I remember some,

INTRODUCTION

it is not the same as having them all written down for future generations to read; to know where they came from.

My cousin Norma Cromwell (Aunt Bonnie's daughter) and I have talked many times about making sure we get those stories recorded. We want these penned histories to be remembered in the future when the elders have passed away. I made a tribute post on my Facebook account about my aunt Bonnie and once again, my friend Tracie commented on the post, saying I should write a book about my parents. She remarked that they clearly had such wonderful memories, pictures, and stories from their childhood, growing up in the Deep South, and these needed to be shared with the world. She went on to say how they were just ordinary people, able to live, survive, and thrive despite all the challenges they had faced over the years.

Tracie has a master's degree in African American studies. While teaching her classes, she noted that the students knew plenty about Dr. Martin Luther King Jr., Booker T. Washington, Rosa Parks, and many others who made their mark in Alabama and United States history. Yet, her students also wanted to hear about ordinary black folks from that time period too. What about them? How did they live? What did they do? What were their challenges and triumphs? I let Tracie know that I was already working on the book thanks to her encouragement.

Considering the experiences my parents have had, their life is far from ordinary, and they definitely have a story to tell. This book serves as a glimpse into Mom and Dad's life over the last seventy-nine and eighty-five years, respectively. They have had some wins and some losses, happy times and sad, but through it all, they have had each other for over fifty-seven years. Do you want to know *How to Live a Long and Fulfilling Life*? Read *Wisdom from Willie* and *Jewels from Jessie* to see how they have been able to do just that. You may be pleasantly surprised that you have exactly what it takes to do the same.

LESSON 1

ALWAYS REMEMBER WHERE YOU CAME FROM AS IT WILL KEEP YOU GROUNDED

WILLIE'S WISDOM

I was born in Nicholsville, Alabama, to Arthur and Mamie Dixon on May 1st, 1938. I am the youngest of six children and was named after my grandfather. My grandparents on my father's side were Willie and Addie Dixon. My mother's parents were Hayward and Olie Hosea. My grandmother Olie was a twin, and her sister's name was Ollie. I was born on the same day as my grandmother Addie.

My grandfather Willie passed away two months after I was born, so I did not get to know him. I sometimes wondered if, being his namesake, I had inherited characteristics from him. My grandmother Addie came to live with us when I was about eight years old. She caused us quite a few whoopings as she would always tell my parents we were being too loud when we were playing. Dad would break out the switch or the belt. Grandmother Addie stayed with us for about five years. While we loved her, we were not sad to see her relocate.

My other grandparents, Hayward and Olie, lived in Theodore, Alabama. My mother, Walter (my brother), and I rode the bus one summer in 1948 down to visit my grandparents. I was about ten years old. That was the first time I had ever ridden on a bus. Of course, we had to ride in the back of the bus because that was how things were back then. The fare was probably about $2.00.

LESSON 1

My father, Arthur, was a sharecropper. My parents raised five kids—three boys: myself, O.G. (his name does not have any other meaning; my parents just named him with letters), Walter, and two girls: Pecola and Bonnie. We had another brother, Jonas, who would have been a year older than me, but he died from pneumonia as a child.

I also had a half-brother, Johnny Prince Dixon, and a half-sister, Georgia Ann Turner. Even though I did not grow up with them, we still kept in touch with each other. All of my siblings have gone on to glory, and I am the last remaining son.

My brother Walter, who we call W.L., and I were the closest because we were only two years apart. My brother always called me Peel (even into adulthood), but interestingly enough, I have no idea why. Growing up, we did typical things kids do. We played games like marbles, and had to share a bike. We were so excited to have that bike that we would get up early (about 5:00 a.m.) to ride every morning before school. It had a light on it, so even though it was dark, we could see.

I went to school until the tenth grade, and then stopped so I could help the family on the farm full-time. W.L. and I both did this. The other siblings were older and were gone by then. This was just something we had to do. We had a responsibility to help the family, especially during the harvest and planting seasons. I did not mind leaving school at all. I enjoyed farming and being out on the land. It gave me a lot of time to spend with my father. He was not a man of many words, but his actions showed how much he cared for his family.

My mother was an easy-going, quiet lady. She would style her hair in braids and wear her housecoats. She did not work outside the home, other than doing washing and ironing for people from time to time. She would make sure we had home-cooked meals for breakfast, lunch, and dinner. Some of my favorite things that she made were her coconut and chocolate cakes. She also made jelly cakes (they were regular cakes but instead of icing, she used jelly to top them). For the most part, whatever my mother cooked, I liked to eat.

Our house had two bedrooms and a kitchen. Mom and Dad had a bedroom, and the boys and girls shared the other. Living was very simple back then. We did not have modern conveniences as we do now, such as telephones and televisions. Even though we did not have a television, we were able to see movies at the local elementary school. There was a man who would set up western movies there on Fridays and me and my brother W.L. would walk to go see them. We only had to pay ten cents for a movie, and it was one of our favorite things to do. Since we only watched westerns, it is no surprise that I still enjoy them to this day. The western channel is one of my favorites.

At home, we did not have electricity. It is probably hard to imagine today, but back then, we used candles and oil kerosene lamps for light at night. The first time I had electricity was when I moved to Mobile at nineteen years old in 1957.

Mom had to wash clothes in a tub with a washboard that had a fire under the tub. She would take the clothes out and rinse them with her hands. We did not have a bathroom either. We took baths in a foot tub and had an outhouse. Fresh drinking

LESSON 1

water came from a well. We would go out into the woods and cut down trees for the stove and fireplace. Sometimes it would get so cold that the entire ground would freeze, and icicles hung off the house. We did not get sick back then, even though it was freezing cold. My mother would do her home remedies. She would make all kinds of teas using liniment.

My dad worked as a logger and a farmer. During the summer, we would work together in the field all day, starting up at daylight. We would come home for lunch and then go back out until around 5:00 p.m. In the summer, we grew sugar cane and would take two wagon loads to the syrup mill to make homemade syrup. It would take three to four hours to cook in the mill. The mill owner received one gallon for every four that we had as payment. By the time we were done, we would have about twenty-five gallons of syrup. We had so much syrup that it would last from one winter to the next.

We also picked corn and we took it to the mill; had it ground up. All we had to do was put it in sacks and bring it home. My mom used it to cook. She also used lard from hogs. We did not really have to buy too much from the store because we grew everything we needed ourselves. When we were old enough, my brother W.L. and I would take out the mules and plow the fields ourselves.

We grew sweet potatoes in the fall. Plowed and pulled them up, then put them atop a bed we'd made out of corn stalks, located out in the woods. We would put straw around the potatoes, and that would ensure they lasted throughout the winter. When we needed some, we would go out into the woods and get some. We could plow up four beds of sweet potatoes at a time.

We had greens, cabbage, onions, tomatoes, corn, sugar cane, sweet potatoes, watermelons, and peas. Some of these, like the greens, cabbage, and peas, we could freeze. These would last about a year. We also had cows for milk and butter, and hogs and chicken for meat. Farming sustained everyone back then.

We had a well where we got our fresh water. We would put our milk and butter in a bucket and lower it down into the well, and when we needed some, we would just pull it up. We smoked the meat in the smokehouse that we had. We smoked hog meat for about three hours. Once the meat smoked, we stored it in the smokehouse. We smoked in the winter, and it would last through the summer months. We bought ice from a man who came around and sold ice. At that time, it cost about fifty cents for fifty pounds of ice which would last us about five days.

We also helped my dad plant cotton. Again, it was another process where the whole family got involved. It was grueling at times to pick cotton because your hands would get cut up. But, we had to keep going. This is what my dad did to support our family. Once a week during harvest season, Dad, W.L., and I would load up the cotton to take to a cotton gin. We would leave around 4:00 a.m., taking an hour-long ride by horse and buggy. Today, it's a very short ride in the car to the gin from where we lived, but by horse and buggy, it took a while.

My dad would earn about $300-$400 for the bales of cotton. In today's currency, that would equal about $1000. We would take about five bales of cotton on each trip to the gin. Once my

LESSON 1

dad was paid, he would pay all his debts, including rent for the land that we lived and farmed on and the groceries and other things we would get from the store.

The gin is still operational today. It is interesting to see a place we went to all those years ago still sitting in the center of our town. My dad stopped farming once we were all grown because he could not maintain the work by himself.

We went to church at Antioch Baptist, using the mule and wagon to travel about two miles from where we lived. Everyone in Nicholsville attended the church as it was the only one in town for black people. All of my family members were included. As life goes, all of them were buried there, too. My parents, grandparents, uncles, and aunts were all placed there when their time came.

As a young boy, I remember that the racial climate was not bad. We did give white men the title of 'mister' when we spoke to them. Some called you by your first name, but many used the N-word. It was wrong, and we knew it, but there was nothing we could do about it because if you pushed back, you could be harmed. They could say it, and you would go on your way so as not to cause trouble. White people also referred to older black men as uncles and older black women as aunts. Of course, none of them were related, but that was just what they did in those days. For us, that was just normal at the time. We knew people were prejudiced, but they did not seem to show it as much in our town. People got along fairly well.

My dad bought his first car in 1950. It was a 1949 black Chevrolet. At the time, not many black people had cars in

Nicholsville. My dad was the oldest child in his family, so he was the first one to get a car when he did. He must have been about forty-seven years old at that time. He had never learned how to drive a car. He bought the car from a black man in Thomasville and that man had to drive him home because my dad was not able to drive. The car was a standard shift, so it took some effort, but that man taught my dad how to drive.

From then on, Dad was able to teach us to as well. W.L. actually wrecked the car six months later. Four people were in the car: myself, J.T. Hudson (our cousin), and Bennon Young (our brother O.G.'s brother-in-law). We tried to tell W.L. that he was going too fast, but he would not listen and hit the gas even more. We were going eighty miles an hour into a curve. He lost control and the car rolled over twice.

Amazingly enough, all of us got out of the car unhurt. When the car rolled over the second time, the door came open, and I fell out. My dad said if the vehicle had rolled over one more time, it would have rolled on me. The accident happened at about 10:00 p.m. A white man came through and asked who our parents were. He knew my dad, so he picked us up and took us home. I thought W.L.'s driving days were over, but Dad let him drive again—even after all of that.

My dad loved to have a little whiskey in his black coffee in the morning. He had a whiskey mill in the woods that he shared with his cousin Eli. Most people called it moonshine during those times. He sold it on and off for many years. He only got caught once, and the police came and arrested him at our house. Someone had turned him in, and this led to a raid of

LESSON 1

both my father's and his cousin Eli's property. My brother W.L. and I had to get him out of jail. My oldest brother, O.G., was caught multiple times selling moonshine as well.

My mother died of ovarian cancer in 1978 at sixty-nine years old. When she was in the hospital, I remember taking my children Willie Jr. and Angela who I will talk more about later, around the back of the hospital to see her. Children were not allowed in the hospital at that time, and I knew my mother would not live long, so I wanted the children to see her one last time. They were able to wave and smile at her through the window. My mother spent her life taking care of the family. Back in those days, in the country, they did not have the treatments available that they do now. My father died in 1984 at eighty years old. He lived a long life and passed from old age. I always remember his favorite outfit, a pair of jean overalls. He wore overalls every day. I still have a pair of them. Those overalls are about seventy-plus years old. I can still wear them, and sometimes I still do, just to remember my dad.

Another interesting story I heard from my father growing up is that our name really was not Dixon. Apparently, our name should have been Davis, but it was changed at some point. No one really explained to me how this happened or even if anyone knew. Of course, there is no one left now that would know, but I just wanted to mention that. I wish I had asked more about that to learn how that came about. So, for those of you reading, if you have elders in your life, try to question them and learn where you came from. It is important to know.

JESSIE'S JEWELS

I was born in Butler, Alabama, to Jesse and Daisy Mae (Hodges) Coleman on January 20th, 1944. I was born at home. I did not find out until years later that my birthday was recorded as January 25th. When you are born in the home, it takes them a few days to record it. They must have noted the date it was recorded, but I still celebrate it on my actual birthday.

My paternal grandparents were Allen and Estella Ray Coleman, and my maternal grandparents were Lloyd and Minnie Hodges. I came from a big family. My mother gave birth to sixteen children, but two died as infants, so there was a total of fourteen living children. I was the fifth child— and the first girl. Growing up with so many siblings was a lot of fun. The first-born was Bennie Charlies (B.C.), then Charlie Lewis (C.L.), Jesse James, Leonard, me, Bessie Mae, Minnie Lee, Johnnie Lee, Robert, Leroy, Shirley Ann, Larry, Bernice, and Lemoral.

I had a good mother. She and my dad married when she was eighteen, and my dad was twenty-four. We had a good life growing up, even though we did not have much. My mother loved to cook. One of the best things she made was tea cakes. They were sort of like vanilla cookies. Her favorite things to make were chicken and dumplings, and sweet potato pies.

I have some fond memories of my grandfather, Grandpa Lloyd. Many of the grandchildren just called him Papa. When I was young, me and my aunt Frankie Cornelius, Papa's daughter, who was two years older than me, would have to go to the store to get fish or other items for Papa. He never sent any money, but we would just go, and Frankie would say Papa needs this or that, and the owner would give us what he wanted, and we would take it home.

One time, we went for some fish and did not get what he wanted because when Frankie told the store owner that Papa wanted these items, the store owner asked about the money, and we did not have any.

When we got back home, Papa said, "Where is the fish?"

"The store owner did not give it to us because we did not have the money," we responded.

"Did you tell them who sent you?"

"Well, Papa…" we said.

He sent us back up there to tell the owner it was Lloyd Hodges who wanted the fish.

When we returned and told the store owner who sent us, the store owner said, "Well, why didn't you say that the first time you were here?"

The store owner filled our tub up with fish, and we went on our way. The same thing would happen with Grandma, Papa's wife, Minnie Hodges. Grandma Minnie would send us to the store with a note. The lady at the store would read it and give us everything listed.

Sometimes there were white people in the store looking at us—these little negro children. I'm sure they were wondering where we came from and how we could get these things without paying. Truth be told, the store owner was my grandmother's half-brother as they shared the same father. They treated my grandmother with respect in that regard and made sure she always had what she needed.

My grandfather was infamous. Everyone (white or black) in the town, knew Grandpa Lloyd. Everyone would call him Uncle Lloyd, and no one messed with him because he never went anywhere without a .45 revolver in his hip pocket, and everyone knew he had it, including family, friends—even the police. Overalls and all, there was the .45. When I say he took it everywhere, I mean it—he even took it to church. Our pastor never said anything about it and carried on with the word of God just like normal.

My grandpa did not mess with anyone, and no one messed with him. Rightfully so. He always said, "Never draw a gun if you don't plan on using it."

I do not remember him having to use his gun, so I assume people just knew to stay in their place around him. Sometimes when people in town went to the police about disputes, they would tell them to go to Uncle Lloyd because he would take care of it, and he did. Grandpa Lloyd lived a long life, all the way to ninety-five years old. Grandma Minnie lived to be about eighty-five.

Everyone loved my mother, Daisy Mae. Unfortunately, we do not have any pictures of her because my children and most

LESSON 1

of my nieces and nephews have never even seen her. Apparently, the only pictures of her were burned in a fire many years ago.

My father, Jesse, was a good man as well. He was smart and very well-liked in the community. We lived on the land of a white man, Arthur Ward, in Choctaw County. For about ten years, our family lived on the land, and my father farmed it. My father decided he wanted to buy a house, and he was able to get a loan based on an acre of land my uncles owned.

When my father told Mr. Ward that he was building a house, Mr. Ward did not believe him, but sure enough, my father did. After the house was built, my father moved it to the land in a town called Butler. I would babysit the Wards' daughter from time to time just to make a little money. You could buy a lot with a few dollars back in those days.

We grew up in the church. My four brothers, Bessie Mae, and I, all got baptized in a lake at the same time. I was nine at the time, and my sister, Bessie Mae, was seven.

Growing up, my mother taught me how to cook, milk cows, and wash clothes. All of us children had to help with the chores. We had two cows, and my dad raised a lot of chickens. My sister Bessie Mae and I would have to pluck and slaughter chickens for dinner. We would put the chicken in an iron kettle, and the feathers would come off quickly. My brother Leonard and I gathered eggs every day from the chicken coop.

We had a dirt yard, so one of our chores was to keep it clean. My brother B.C. would cut dogwood trees with big green leaves, and we would put them together and make brooms to sweep the yard. My sister Bessie Mae and I swept the yard every Saturday.

We were happy in those days. We picked cotton every day except Saturday and Sunday. My brothers would pick 100 pounds, and sometimes I would pick thirty to fifty pounds. We picked cotton all day. Even though the school year had started, we could not go until about a month later because we had to pick the cotton. We would also pick blackberries and make pies from them. Sometimes, we'd also make plum jelly and would sell it to make some spending money. We loved to fish and play ball. We loved Christmas time. Our parents would give each of us a shoebox filled with fruit, candy, and raisins. We always had a lot of fruit since my dad worked at the IGA food store. He would take a foot tub to the store and collect any fruit that had a little bruising and bring it home. My dad also worked at a fish market cleaning fish, so we had a lot of fish too.

My sister Bessie Mae and I also sold candy for spending money. I used some of it to buy my first cancan hoop skirt, one you would wear under your dress. Back then, that was all the rave, and all the girls had one. A cancan hoop skirt would make your dress stand out. We spent a lot of time visiting our grandparents, aunts, and cousins. I remember my aunt, Vera Mae, could make the best biscuits around.

When I was in the seventh and eighth grades, I was a cheerleader and ran track. In high school, I was a good student, although I did not do many extracurricular activities. On Fridays, Bessie Mae and I would go to the dance at a local store. We had dance contests, and whoever won would get a prize. I once won one dollar and some flower handkerchiefs.

A dollar could buy a lot at that time. I decided to enter the contest. A song by Booker T and the MG called Green Onions was on, so I made up a dance. I think it compares to the electric slide, but going forward and backward, instead of side to side. The winner was picked by the older kids, and they picked me. Those were fun times.

As a side note, later, I will tell you more about my daughter Angela. If you know her, you know that she wins a lot. You can see she gets it from her momma!

When I was in the ninth grade, I went to stay with my grandmother Estella, my dad's mother. I stayed with her for three years. She lived about twenty minutes away from us. This was a family tradition because my father always sent one child to stay with his mother after her husband Allen was killed and her second husband Sam passed.

My grandfather Allen had gone to get seeds to plant his garden and was shot because a man was upset that my grandfather chastised him on church grounds for using bad language. Thankfully they knew who the guy was, and he went to prison. My grandmother remarried a man named Sam Adkins. He took care of my uncles, who were still young at the time, and raised them like his own.

Grandmother Estella did not want me to do anything fun. All I could do was watch the Ed Sullivan show. She did not want me to go out anywhere, either. I stayed there until I graduated from Choctaw County Training high school in 1963. When I was in the twelfth grade, in our yearbook, they wrote that I had million-dollar legs because I had big pretty legs. I would get teased all the time after that because people would ask me to see those million-dollar legs. Sometimes I would show them, and sometimes, I did not!

My grandmother did not want me to leave Butler when I graduated, so we went to my parent's home because she said she wanted to see what my father had to say about me leaving. My grandmother told my father that I wanted to go to Mobile, and my mother chimed in that if I wanted to go, I could. My father did not say a word about that. My mother always spoke up for what we wanted, and my father never gave her any pushback. The church and my relatives gave me money for graduation. I had about twenty-five dollars and took the bus from Butler to Mobile. My cousins wanted me to come to Birmingham, but I did not like the city, so Mobile it was.

When I left, the next in line was my sister Bessie Mae, but she did not go stay with my grandmother because my mother needed her to stay at home. So, my sister Minnie Lee was sent to stay with our grandmother instead. Minnie Lee was there for two years until the house burned down. After that time, my uncles took my grandmother to Birmingham to live with them.

My mother died on September 3rd, 1967. She was only forty-eight years old. She died the same year my first child was born. She was pregnant with her last child, a girl, and died during childbirth. My father passed away in 1979 at the age of sixty-six. I have also lost my brothers B.C., C.L., Leonard, Johnnie Lee, Jessie James, Robert, Leroy, and my sister Minnie Lee. I am blessed to still have one aunt on my dad's side Clorine Weston who is our first centenarian at 100 years old and two aunts and an uncle on my mom's side Frankie Cornelius, Willie Brundage and Jessie Hodges.

Walter, left and Willie Sr. as children growing up in Nicholsville, Alabama.

Mamie Dixon, Willie Sr.'s mother, was a homemaker who made sure the family had what they needed. She was a gentle and kind soul to all.

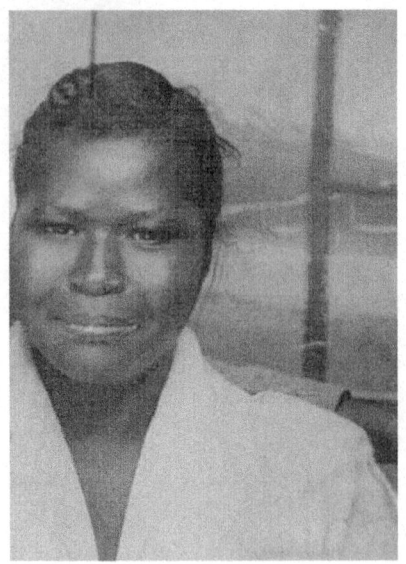

Sibling Pecola Dixon Barron as a young woman.

Arthur Dixon, Willie's father, seen here in his later years of life. He worked as a logger and sharecropper.

Siblings: Bonnie Richardson and Johnnie Dixon at a family gathering in Alabama.

These pictures are of the gin company Willie Sr., and his father Arthur and brother Walter would go to and sell their cotton. The gin is still operational today.

Siblings: Bonnie Richardson and Willie, Sr. at her 92nd birthday party in 2021.

Jessie's high school graduation picture.

Coleman Siblings: Jesse James, Jessie Mae, Bennie Charles and Leroy Coleman saying goodbye to brother Charlie Lewis.

Coleman sisters: Jessie Mae, Bessie Mae, Bernice, Shirley Ann, Cherry (sister-in-law) and Minnie Lee, seated visiting for Minnie's birthday in Mississippi.

Coleman Siblings: Larry, Bessie Mae, Bernice, Lemoral, Shirley Ann and Jessie Mae all together after saying goodbye to sister Minnie.

Coleman Siblings: Jessie Mae, Johnnie Lee and Bessie Mae at Johnnie's wedding.

Coleman Siblings: Leroy, Lemoral, Larry and Robert

Willie's older brother Walter Dixon a.k.a. W.L.

Willie Sr's brother O.G., the first born of the Dixon children.

Willie Sr's grandmother, Olie Hosea.

Jessie's father Jesse Coleman who worked as a sharecropper. He raised his family to be strong and tight knit.

Willie Sr., wearing his dad's overalls that are over 70 years old.

Jessie's grandfather Allen Coleman and grandmother Estelle Coleman on her dad's side.

Jessie's grandfather Lloyd Hodges and grandmother Minnie Hodges on her mother's side.

Coleman sibling Charlie Lewis Coleman

Coleman sibling Leonard Coleman

Jessie and her aunt Clorine Weston who is the family's first centenarian celebrating 100 years.

LESSON 2

YOUTH IS FOR LEARNING; YOU DON'T HAVE TO GET EVERYTHING RIGHT, BUT YOU CAN LEARN FROM EVERYTHING YOU DO

WILLIE'S WISDOM

I had remained at home in Nicholsville helping with the farming, but it got to be too much for Dad; he stopped doing that work. I left home at nineteen in 1957 and moved to Mobile to work. I stayed with my cousins Prumis and Annie Gray Dixon for about three months. My sister Bonnie and brother W.L. got an apartment, so we all stayed together for a few years. W.L. had been in Mobile for four years, so he was working.

Once W.L. got married, I moved in with him and his wife, Minnie, for about five years. It was a nice arrangement because I helped out with the household chores and always made sure their cars were clean. I was good at washing cars early on, and it would become a pastime for me for many years.

I bought my first car, a 1956 powder blue Ford, after I got a job. My first job in Mobile was in the construction business, building houses. Later, a man told me about a job at a furniture store in Prichard, Alabama, with the Wilson family, so I applied and was hired. I worked there for years. When Mr. Wilson sold the store to Rhodes Furniture, he told them to make sure they kept me on. They did, and I stayed there for six years until I got a job working the toll for the Mobile Transit in 1969.

As young adults, we would mostly go to the movies on the weekend. Movies were only fifty cents. They mainly showed

LESSON 2

westerns, and we saw many of them. We only had to pay a dime for a drink, hotdog, and burger. Things were very cheap. Even though we did not make much money, we were still able to enjoy these fun things.

We did not go anywhere else except to visit our parents back home in Nicholsville and later, after they moved, to Dixon Mills. We visited home every other weekend. Considering we were so happy to leave home and be out on our own, we visited a lot to spend time with family and eat some of mom's good home cooking.

One of the scariest times for me was one day when I got off work from the furniture store in 1961. I had just gotten my Christmas check—all $50 of it—and went to the bank to cash it. After I left the bank, I went over to the furniture store. Two guys who were standing at the corner approached me, said they had guns, and told me to get into their car. I assumed they had been watching me and knew I had money.

I did not see any guns, but one of them said he had a gun in his pocket, and I had no reason not to believe it was not true. I had no idea who those guys were as I had never seen them before. They had me get in the front seat, and sit between them. We drove around for less than an hour. During the ride, they did not say much. They just told me not to tell anyone and not to go to the police, or they would come back for me.

After that, they dropped me back off at the store and made me give them all of the money I had. Suffice it to say, I never called the police and only told my brother what had happened. I never spoke about it with anyone else, until now. I never saw those two again after that day, and I am thankful for that. Even though this was a traumatic experience, and it scared me, I wanted to keep my job, keep working, and progress. So, I kept moving forward. I knew, as a good person, that I would have more good days than bad ones like that one.

♥ ♥ ♥ ♥

LESSON 2

JESSIE'S JEWELS

I rode the bus to Mobile in 1963 to get a job and stayed with my brother B.C. and his wife Inez and their two children, Gloria and Daphne, for about three years. I wanted to go to college to become a nurse, but my family could not afford it. So, I found a job as a waitress at a restaurant called the Oyster House on Davis Avenue.

I loved my job there and worked until the restaurant closed. I also sent what I could afford back home to my parents to help them out. We only made about twenty-one dollars a week, and I would still send my parents about ten dollars of that. I was able to get another job at a barbeque restaurant after the Oyster House closed.

My best friends were Johnnie Ward and Sarah Longmire. Johnnie is Inez's sister, but everyone thought Johnnie and I were sisters. If she had a dime, I would have a nickel of it. I met Sarah because she married my high school classmate, Levi Horne. Sarah and I are still the best of friends today.

As young adults, for fun, we would go to the Booker-T theater and sometimes we would go to the fair down on Davis Avenue. We went to church at Greater Mount Olive Baptist Church #2. Rosie Kaye Knighton, Inez's sister, stayed around the corner from the church, so we would go over to her house and walk with her to church. We would go to downtown Mobile every weekend. We walked or took the bus everywhere we went. We went to stores including Lerner's, Webbers, Woolworths, and Crest. At Woolworths, they had a lunch counter where we could sit and eat in the store.

While we did not have much, we enjoyed each other and had a good time with family and friends. Mobile was a great place for me to live as a young person, and I am glad that I moved there to start my adult life.

Willie, Sr. around 19 years old when he moved to Mobile.

Jessie in her 20s enjoying her time in Mobile.

LESSON 3

MARRIAGE AND PARENTING IS A PROCESS, JUST STAY THE COURSE AND DO THE BEST YOU CAN

JESSIE'S JEWELS

Marriage is something that you have to work at. We had good examples from our parents, who showed us that marriage requires sacrifice and hard work. We have been married for fifty-seven years. For us, the key to staying married is knowing that we love and respect each other. No matter what happens, we know that we can work through it together.

You have to understand each other, and you have to give some and take some. There will be times when you have to negotiate and allow things to go both ways, so each one is happy. It will not be peachy every day, but you take it one day at a time. We have never been a couple to run the streets or anything like that. Some people have to deal with that, but I could not be bothered with it, so I am glad Willie was not that type of person.

I met Willie after about a month of working at the Oyster House in 1963. I was nineteen at the time, and he was twenty-five. We didn't start dating until 1964. I was working at the restaurant, and most people who would come in there came by themselves. They either order and eat at the counter or order and get it to go.

One day, Willie came in and sat at a table in the dining room. He ordered smothered chicken and vegetables. Yes, I still remember his meal. I seated him at a table for two.

I asked him, "Where is your girlfriend?"

"I don't have one," he replied.

When he was done eating, I brought the check.

"Where is your boyfriend?" he asked, and I said I did not have one.

He paid his check and asked what time I got off.

"11:00 p.m.," I said.

He said he would come back and take me home from work.

I said, "Well if you want to."

He said he would be across the street, but I did not see him when I left work that night. So, I walked home because the house was just around the corner from the restaurant. I was still staying with my brother B.C. at the time. Willie came there to pick me up, but I did not see him, so he went home. From that day forward, Willie would come to the restaurant for a meal when I was at work.

The Oyster House restaurant eventually closed, so I did not see Willie for a while until one day, I was getting ready to catch the bus to go downtown with my friend Marie to shop with the tips I had earned. We had five more minutes waiting on the bus. When we looked up, Willie was driving up in his black Chevrolet. He was off that day. We told him we were going to town, and he said he was too, so he gave us a ride.

He asked me again what time I was getting off from work and if he could pick me up. At this time, I was working at Ella's Barbeque. I said yes and told him the time. He came back that afternoon to pick me up at 11:00 p.m. and, from then on, picked me up from work every night. Sometimes we would go by a restaurant called Oasis to get hamburgers and milkshakes. It was a drive-in, so you could order and then eat there in your car. I used to eat so much barbeque and fish where I worked, so this was a welcome change.

I remember one time while we were dating, I went home to visit my parents in Butler and rode with our friend Levi Horne. Willie came up there to get me. We were going to tell my parents that we were planning on getting married. My sister Shirley was ten years old at the time, and I told her that I was going to play a joke on Willie. When he came in, my sisters told him that I was already gone.

"Oh no! She ain't gone back, and I done come way up here," he yelled out.

After he said that, I walked out and surprised him, and we all burst into laughter. My parents felt that Willie was a nice guy, and they gave their blessing.

On March 2nd, 1966, we got married at the courthouse after two years of dating. It was a Wednesday, and it was Willie's off day. My brother B.C. was our witness. I wore a blue two-piece suit, and Willie wore a shirt, pants, and tie. We spent the first few nights with my in-laws, W.L., and his wife, Minnie.

Shortly after, we moved into a small house at the corner of the street W.L. and Minnie stayed on. W.L. and Minnie had a small reception for us on a Saturday night with some family and friends, including Annie Gray, Prumis Dixon, and Hollis, and Johnnie Mosely.

Willie introduced Johnnie to her husband, Hollis. Willie worked with Hollis at the furniture store, and Hollis was looking

LESSON 3

for a nice lady. We invited Hollis and Johnnie over to our place for dinner one night. It took Hollis a while to get there, but he finally made it, and they hit it off. They ended up dating and getting married a few years later.

So, that is how we began. We have been married for over fifty-seven years. It's not always peaches and cream, but when you love each other, you can make it work. We just know each other's ways. All is well, and we just like each other's company and being around one another. We thank the Lord for that.

Over the years, we have had some great times, and of course, some sad times. We just take each day as they come. We do not judge each other. Sometimes we have disagreements and discussions, but all in all, we know that each of us always has the other's best interest in mind.

We had our first child together on July 8th, 1967—Willie Jr. He was a good son. He did not give us any trouble and did well in school. Growing up, Willie Jr. was very active in the band. He played the trombone at Sidney Phillips Middle School and at John L. LeFlore High School. In high school, Willie Jr. played basketball too. He was tall—six-foot-one inch. He took after my brothers in that regard. They were all tall as well. He and I had something in common, too, as we both were left-handed.

Willie Jr. grew up with the neighborhood kids playing basketball and baseball. He loved going to the neighborhood boys' club and was a boy of the year for two years in a row. Some of his best friends were Marty Cunningham and Marlon Gover. They were good kids growing up. They never got into any bad trouble.

Willie Jr. worked selling newspapers when he was a sophomore in high school. He also worked at a grocery store, stocking shelves and taking people's groceries out to their cars. When he finished high school in 1986, Willie Jr. went to Alabama State University on a band scholarship. There, he met another good friend, Marcus Lewis, who had the same major as him in Communications.

Willie Jr. earned a bachelor's degree and completed his studies in the summer of 1992. His graduation was held in May 1993 because the school did not have a fall graduation. Willie Sr. and I have always been very proud of him. He was the first in our family to graduate from college. We never had the chance to go to college, so it was a proud moment. I always wanted to go to college and become a nurse, but I was not able to once I started a family. Having him graduate was a big accomplishment for our family.

Willie Jr. got a job with a local television station when he graduated and worked there until he got married to Dorothy Brown in 1994. He left and moved to Moline, Illinois, then Orlando, Florida, and worked for Channel 9, an ABC affiliate. He worked there for eleven years before moving to Houston, Texas, to work for another ABC affiliate, Channel 13. Willie Jr. went to visit Houston and saw that he could have his dream home with a pool, and this sold him on moving. He and Dorothy have two daughters, Dominique and Sydney.

Sadly, we lost Willie Jr. on April 25th, 2020, from a blood clot in his legs. We miss him greatly.

Our daughter Angela was born on August 22nd, 1971, just four years after Willie Jr. She was a shy girl but very smart and always a good student. She was very active in school activities. She participated in the student newspaper in middle school. In high school, she was the recording secretary for the student council. She also played clarinet in the band and was a member of the National Honor Society and other clubs as well.

During her senior year, she wrote the class song. She even tried out for the Azalea Trail Maids, who are considered ambassadors to the city. Even though she was not selected, it was the first time that girls from John. L. LeFlore High School participated. She was also selected as Ms. LeFlore and represented the school during the year. She was in the Upward Bound Program at Spring Hill College. Upward Bound is a program to help first-generation students prepare for college. She initially went to Stillman College on a scholarship and then transferred to Alabama A&M University in Huntsville, Alabama. She earned a scholarship there and was always on the Dean's List. She finished with a Bachelor of Arts degree in English and a minor in Political Science.

After graduation, Angela got a job with the Department of the Army, working in Public Affairs. She worked for the government for seven years, all while earning a master's degree from St. Ambrose University. Later, she decided to go to law school at the University of Iowa College of Law. After graduation, she took the Texas Bar exam, passed it on the first try, and became an attorney. That was a goal she'd had since high school. She worked for a law firm for two years and then started her own practice. She worked as a parking judge in municipal court for two years during that time. She now handles cases for school districts and government entities.

Willie Jr. and Angela both liked reading and watching television. One of their favorite shows was the Jackson 5 show. Willie Jr. was a good eater too, but Angela was very picky. She loved McDonald's, and when she did not want what I cooked, Willie Sr. would go there and get her a burger and fries.

When Willie Jr. first went to college, he would call every day until he was settled. Angela did a little better than he did on that.

Those were the good old days. After they grew up and left the nest, they were out on their own. It was nice to know they could support themselves, but we still miss them a lot. They would call and come home when they could.

♥ ♥ ♥ ♥

LESSON 3

WILLIE'S WISDOM

My first son was born when I was twenty-three years old from a previous relationship. Brent was born on April 4th, 1964. I met his mother in Mobile. The first time I saw him, he was about a month or so old. Growing up, I did not see him a lot. I guess after getting married and having more children, and working, I thought it was better to support him from afar. Over the years, after Brent became an adult, we formed a better relationship. I am glad about that.

I was able to go to his wedding, where he married Felicia Hudson and attended family birthdays. Brent has a son named Brandon and a daughter named Shantora. They have grandchildren as well. Over the years, they have come over to visit, and we have had good chats and good times with one another. I am thankful that we have been able to spend time with Brent and Felicia. Felicia always makes us such nice items like shirts and pillows to remember family members who have passed on. She made shirts with my mom and dad's pictures on them and gave them to me. These are still items that I cherish and love to wear.

Willie Sr., and Jessie enjoying time together visiting family.

Willie Sr., Angela and Willie Jr. enjoying a Sunday afternoon.

Angela, 6 and Willie Jr., 10

Dixon Family portrait taken at church after Easter service.

Willie Jr. on a trip to Six Flags with Charles Barkley in the picture.

Felicia, Brent, Angela and Willie, Sr. at Brent's 40th birthday party.

Willie Jr., Angela and Brent

LESSON 4

IN LIFE, YOU MUST WORK TO LIVE, NOT LIVE TO WORK

WILLIE'S WISDOM

My first job was for Wilson's home furniture store in Prichard. I delivered furniture all over the city with my co-worker David Lucas. It was hard but honest work. I made twenty-five dollars a week. Later, my pay was raised to thirty dollars a week. Back then, that was good money because things were so cheap. I delivered furniture for twelve to fourteen hours a day. Eventually, that store was sold and became Rhodes Furniture. I continued working there and had my pay raised again to forty dollars a week. They paid overtime, and sometimes, I could make up to sixty dollars in a week. Sometimes we would deliver furniture out of town.

In 1969, I started working for a bus company called National City Line. National City eventually closed down. The city took it over and renamed it Mobile Transit. They could not hire everyone to drive the bus at the time, so I worked at Bankhead tunnel, collecting tolls for a year and a half.

Once the city bought more buses, I was able to go back and work for Mobile Transit. I worked there for over forty-five years. I was a full-time bus driver from 1972 to 2003 and a part-time driver from 2004 to 2016. I also drove charter buses for many years, taking people on regional trips to the casinos and beaches in Florida and Mississippi.

LESSON 4

When I first started working for the city bus in the 1970s, I made $1.60 an hour. At the time, there were very few black drivers, and passengers did not always treat us well. Some passengers did not even want to ride with black drivers, but the administration did not stand for that. When white passengers would demand that they remove the black driver from a route, Mobile Transit would push back and say you can either ride the bus with the drivers we choose, or walk.

Many days I would drive the bus twelve to fourteen hours a day. As time went on, the wages increased. In the 1980s, I made twelve dollars an hour. In the 1990s, it was increased to fifteen an hour.

My work hours were very early. I would rise at 4:00 a.m. and leave for work by 5:00 a.m. It made for some long days, but it was good and honest work. I enjoyed working and often did overtime, so that is how I was able to earn a good living.

I suppose I had what most people today describe as multiple streams of income. In addition to the bus route, I would sometimes help out my friend with his cleaning business for some additional income. During the 1970s, I worked as an overnight security guard, in office buildings as well as at the Alabama shipyard.

During my years as a bus driver, I experienced some very, scary situations. The most frightening occurred in the early 1980s. My first run was at 5:00 a.m. on Saturdays, driving the route between the transit center and downtown. The day this occurred, I was driving Brookley to highway 45, then, stopped to board a passenger at highway 45 and First Avenue.

The police had a roadblock there in an attempt to stop a car. The car drove through the roadblock. Police fired at the vehicle, and two bullets hit the front of the bus I was driving, shattering the headlights. I had to call the supervisor after it happened, and they sent another bus. I simply carried on, continuing on schedule until my shift was up.

Another incident occurred when I was on the Prichard and Eight Mile route. I was leaving downtown and turning on St. Francis and Washington Avenue when a fight broke out on the bus. I had to pull over and stop the fight. A man was attacking a young lady on the long seat in the back. The man had her held down and was beating her with his fists. I went to the back and asked the man to let her go. Thankfully, he did.

There was another time when I was leaving Prichard for Eight Mile; I traveled down the main street to Garrison Avenue. A passenger was at the stop waiting on the bus. Before I could stop the bus, the passenger ran in front of the bus, and I hit her. She fell back, and the bus ran over her. At that point, only her head and chest were visible. She was under the bus and passed out.

Someone called the police and the ambulance as well. They came and picked her up and took her to the hospital. We never heard anything else after that. Every day when I came to work after that for a few weeks, I would ask if they had heard anything about the girl. I wanted to know what had happened to her and how she was doing. I could not believe she did not sue the bus company because she had been run over and hurt. I do not know if she was on drugs or mentally unstable, but it

LESSON 4

surprised me that we never heard anything about what happened to her.

In 1981, a tragedy occurred in Mobile. Michael Donald, a young black man, was hung from a tree by members of the Ku Klux Klan. Sometime later, I realized his mother, Ms. Beulah Mae Donald, was a regular customer on my bus. I did not know who she was until after her son was killed. When she got on the bus, passengers would offer their condolences, saying how sorry they were.

It was a sad time in Mobile. I never really talked to her but just listened to the conversations on the bus from the many passengers. She was a very strong woman to endure that tragedy. She continued to work and move forward while fighting for justice for her son's death for many years.

Over the years, I saw all kinds of characters on the bus. Some were nice, some not so. Some were happy, and others were just sad and mean, but I transported them to where they needed to go either way. Some got on the bus and did not have all the fare, but I would still let them ride from time to time and, sometimes, even put my own money in on their behalf. Many would make up for those times later when they could afford to.

The passengers became like family and friends to me because they rode daily, to and from work, or wherever else they needed to go. Some talked and shared what was going on in their lives, and others just rode in silence to wherever they were going. Some were loud, others soft-spoken, but they were all just regular people like me, trying to make it.

In the 1980s, I started participating in the Bus Rodeo, which was a yearly competition for bus drivers where we would drive the bus through an obstacle course. The winner represented the city at the national competition. I participated because first place won an all-expenses-paid trip to the nationals.

We had to drive with precision through the course. We could not touch the cones, had to turn corners with the appropriate space, and ended the course in a sprint, stopping the bus just before the final cone. I must admit, I was very good at driving a bus, so the bus rodeo certainly put my skills to the test.

I won the local competition many times. The first time I was in the rodeo was in 1983, and I won second place, which came with a trophy. I won first place in 1985 and went on a trip to Los Angeles, California, to compete in the national competition. For first place, I won a trophy and $200. I also got a week of paid time off to attend the national competition.

The next year, I won first place and a trip to Atlanta, Georgia. The third trip was to San Francisco, California. The fourth trip I won was to Montreal, Canada. The last time I won first place was a trip to New Orleans, Louisiana. All in total, I came in first place five times and second place twice.

The competition had about 100 drivers. One year, I placed fifth in the national competition, so I was quite proud of that. The national bus rodeo competition was a week-long event with different outings, lunches, and programs. Bus drivers came from all over the country to compete.

I learned that many of the drivers were allowed to continue to practice until the national competition. My transit system

LESSON 4

did not allow that. Everybody who attended had a good time meeting fellow drivers from all over the United States. The bus rodeo was an exciting time. Jessie and I were able to travel to places we had never been before. We even took our daughter Angela with us on the trip to San Francisco. She was sixteen at the time, and that was her first time riding on a plane.

I retired in 2003 after over thirty years of driving for the city bus. After a while, I decided to go back on a part-time basis and drive the lift buses that picked people up from their homes and took them to specific destinations. To ride the lifts, people had to have some sort of disability or be elderly. I did this up until they ended the routes I was driving, finally closing out my career as a driver at age seventy-eight.

♥ ♥ ♥ ♥

JESSIE'S JEWELS

I had several jobs when I came to Mobile in 1963. I began working at the laundry the first week I arrived, folding clothes. I stayed there for a few months and then went to work as a waitress in a family-owned restaurant called the Oyster House. I worked there from August to December, and it closed because the owner got behind on his taxes. New owners took over the restaurant and turned it into a club, so I went back to the laundry and worked there for another month.

A lady named Ms. Williams, who lived next door to us, worked as a cook at Ella's Barbeque and asked if I knew anyone that wanted to work. I told her that I did, so she told Ms. Ella that I would make a great waitress. The restaurant made all the good stuff—fried fish, chicken, barbeque, greens, fries, etc. Ella had me call the restaurant, and I went down for an interview. It went well, and I got the job.

The restaurant was on Davis Avenue, which is now called Martin Luther King Avenue. I worked there until I got married. I did not work for a while after that. Later, I worked at a bank for four hours on the night shift and also, for a cleaning service that was owned by one of the ministers of my church. We cleaned the First National Bank, but I only worked for a short time. I also worked for two years as the caregiver of a young baby.

LESSON 4

Some years later, I worked downtown at the Dog House. The Dog House was a restaurant that sold all types of hot dogs with different toppings. It was very popular and close to a junior college, so the students made up most of our business. Sometimes, many of the students would not have enough for a hot dog and drink. I knew they were working hard in school, so I would just give them a free drink to go with their meal. I worked there for about two years until that location closed.

I also worked for the Mobile school system for a while, in the cafeteria. I closed out my working career for Dr. Timothy and Betsy String, doing many years of days' work (housekeeping), and they treated me like family and still do to this day.

♥ ♥ ♥ ♥

Willie, Sr., displaying his 2nd place in the bus rodeo trophy.

Willie, Sr., after winning first place in the bus rodeo.

Willie Sr., at the national business rodeo competition.

Display of trophies from the bus rodeo competitions.

Willie at the national bus rodeo competition with a Mr. T impersonator.

LESSON 5

YOU MAY NOT HAVE A LOT, BUT ALWAYS SAVE SOMETHING. SAVING NOW MAY SAVE YOU LATER

WILLIE'S WISDOM

Driving the bus, I met some interesting people. There was a pharmacist who rode the bus back in the 1980s. I did not know his real name, but I called him Doc. I picked him up every morning to take him to work downtown. One day, he started talking to me about putting money away for my future. He recommended that I start saving money on a Certificate of Deposit (CD). During that time, CDs were paying five to six percent interest. I took his advice.

He also told me that if I were to save a bit more, I could start putting money in a money market account. This is how I started to save a "right smart" of money. I always say right smart, and it means a good amount. I am not sure where that term came from. He said if you do not have to use the money right away, your money can earn you more money. That was a good lesson to learn. You can start with whatever you can afford, and save.

With CDs, you have to keep the money in the account for about twelve, eighteen, or twenty-four months. Then, when it matures, you start earning interest. Money markets are long-term accounts, so you can make more doing that. Most times, people do not have money for the long term, so if you're looking to start somewhere as I was, the CDs worked well. Back

LESSON 5

then, you could earn more interest. Nowadays, people invest in the stock market, and that is too complicated for me to learn at this stage in my life. But, I am glad I learned to invest in the way that worked for me at the time.

♥ ♥ ♥ ♥

JESSIE'S JEWELS

We taught our children the importance of saving at a young age. When they were growing up, we laid a foundation so they would know the value of saving. We opened up Christmas Club accounts at the beginning of the year, and each payday, I would deposit an amount toward the balance. Our children had their own checking account register so they would note how much they had and could watch it grow week to week. Our children never asked if they could have some of the money early because they understood that the money was for Christmas. They knew that at the end of the year, we would withdraw the money for them, and they could spend it on whatever they wanted.

So, no matter what you make, save something from it. These lessons helped to guide our children's financial life. Angela still uses a bank register to this day, just as we do, because we prefer to document what we are spending. We know there is technology available, but we like the old-fashioned way.

If you have not been saving, start now. Here are some tips:

1. **Save Something.** There is no need to focus on a percentage; five, ten percent, etc. Just save something. Whether it's one dollar or five dollars, it all adds up. The key to saving is putting it somewhere that you cannot have easy access to it.

There are online savings accounts, credit unions, and banks that are there for your convenience. If the money is automatically deducted from your main account to a savings account, you do not have to think about it. If you prefer to get a piggy bank, and yes, they still have those, do that and save the money at home. Just start saving something and do not spend it.

2. **Eliminate one non-essential expense.** During this time when many are still working from home, it is very likely that you have not been able to get that daily coffee, lunch, or other items you tend to spend money on without even thinking. Use this time to reevaluate how and what you are spending money on. By eliminating at least one expense, you can send that money to your savings account and watch it grow.

3. **Negotiate or cancel recurring bills.** Now is a good time to examine the services you use, like the phone, cable, memberships, subscriptions, etc. You may be paying for something that you are not using. If so, eliminate or negotiate that bill, and instead of spending the money, add it to your savings account.

4. **Set a Savings Goal.** Having a specific goal can offer some motivation for saving. It is important to save for a rainy day, but if identifying a reason like a purchase, paying off a credit card, loans, buying a house, or even a vacation helps you save, then do that. Just remember not to use all of your savings for that purpose. The important point here is to always leave an amount in the savings fund and continue to build on it.

While there are countless ways to save, these are just a few suggestions to get you started and on your way. Saving gives you a sense of security in times of uncertainty and allows you to maintain your lifestyle without the need to seek help from others. While we all need help sometimes, now is the time to be more aware of how you can help yourself over the long term.

♥ ♥ ♥ ♥

LESSON 6

OWNING A HOME SHOULD BE A GOAL. IF YOU DESIRE TO HAVE ONE, YOU MUST PLAN, SAVE, AND ACT

WILLIE'S WISDOM

When we first got married in 1966, we lived in a house on the same street as my brother W.L. The house had two bedrooms and one bathroom. Strangely enough, it did not have a face bowl, just a toilet, and a shower. The house was about 500 square feet. We only lived there for less than a year. After that, we moved into an apartment for about a year.

Later, we moved into a house on Dubose Street. The house was owned by the Wilsons, who ran the furniture store where I worked. They asked if I wanted to buy the house, but I did not want to as it was not the type of house that I wanted. It was too close to the street, did not have a yard, and stood too high off the ground with a long staircase in the back.

We had a scary moment there one day with Jessie and Angela. They were walking out of the door, and Angela almost fell down the stairs. Jessie had to pull her so hard to keep her from falling that she pulled her arm out of place. We knew then that we did not want to buy the Wilsons' house, but we continued to rent for $40 a month and lived there for about four to five years.

We decided to start looking for a house to buy in 1973. Our children were small when we bought our own. Willie Jr. was six, and Angela was two. We drove around looking for houses,

LESSON 6

and when we saw the house that we were interested in, I called the realtor. He let us in to look at it. Another couple showed up also wanting the house, but because we were there first, we were able to apply first. We completed an application, and because I had good credit, I was able to get approved for a loan. The house note was $70 a month. Having good credit is key to being able to make large purchases.

The total cost of the house was about $11,000. We were able to move in after a month. The neighborhood was mixed with white and black families when we moved in. There were no issues or problems at the time, but eventually, most of the white families moved out, and the neighborhood became occupied by mostly black families.

A neighborhood is made up of those you live around. We have had some good neighbors, such as Florence Turner, Willie Taylor, Deacon Earnest, and Juanita Bee, Joe Aldridge, Lindsay, and Louise George, Betty Richardson, Carolyn, and Bobby Gover, Eugene and Charlene Phillips, James and Jane Montgomery, James Franklin, the George's, the Carstarphen's and more. Over the years, we have supported each other and treated each other well. We are more like family than neighbors, and it really makes a difference to have people around with values and ideals similar to your own.

Our house had three bedrooms, but we turned one into a den, so the children had to share a room for many years. Eventually, we added a separate den to the home and were able to give Willie Jr. and Angela their own rooms. Our home has provided us with safety and shelter for many years. Being a homeowner comes with a lot of responsibilities because when something goes wrong with the home, you have to get things fixed. You have to maintain your property. There have been some natural disasters over the years that have affected us and our home.

Living in Mobile, we have had our share of hurricanes. One of the most serious was hurricane Frederic which made landfall on September 12th, 1979, as a category three. Many people evacuated, but we chose to ride out the storm. We really could not sleep that night, and everyone stayed in one room. The next morning, we got up to survey the damage. There were trees and power lines down everywhere. Shingles from houses had been thrown about. Thankfully, all of our neighbors were fine. That hurricane did so much damage to the city that we were without electricity for two weeks. We had damage to our own home, but it was mainly just on the roof.

One of the bright spots to come out of this situation was that neighbors helped each other in any way they could. On Fridays, I would plug our little black and white television into the car outlet and set out the benches from our picnic table. All the neighbor kids would come over to watch the Dukes of Hazzard. The Dukes of Hazzard was a popular television show during that time. We had a gas stove, so Jessie was able to cook food, and we would all just join in and share. This is one reason we have always kept a gas stove—so that even without electricity, we are always able to cook.

We also had some major storms that caused flooding. There were some floods in 1980 and 1981 where the water rose so high that we had to leave the house. A dam broke in the area,

LESSON 6

and the creek behind us overflowed. We did not have anywhere to go as it was the middle of the night, so we all got in the car and drove further down the street. We were not the only ones; quite a lot of families were doing the same thing. We all lined up along the streets, trying to keep safe. We stayed in the car throughout the night.

Our house was flooded when we returned. Our carpet was ruined, along with some other items in the home, but everything was replaceable. It was just important that we were all safe. The neighborhood always used to be quiet, but it changed as the years passed. Many of those who were here when we first moved in have passed on.

Owning a home comes with challenges, but it is very rewarding as well. After a hard day of work, you can come home to your own place where it is safe and comfortable.

♥ ♥ ♥ ♥

JESSIE'S JEWELS

Having a home has been wonderful, but like Willie said, we have experienced some challenges as well. One of the scariest moments happened back in the early 1980s. It was night, and we had all gone to bed. Willie and I stayed up talking. All of a sudden, we heard a screeching noise and a big bang on one side of the house. Willie went outside and found a car had crashed into the side of our house.

There was a song that came out that same year by a British group called The Madness. Their song, "Our House in the Middle of the Street," described our house. It was in the middle of the street. The driver came barreling down the street, lost control, and ran into the side of the house. The car hit the corner of the house, and the brick side of the wall fell completely off.

The next thing we knew, the police and news media were all over the place. Willie was interviewed by the news station. We had a few minutes of fame, but we did not want it that way. The car hit the side of the room by Willie Jr.'s bed, so we are thankful it did not actually enter the house.

After that ordeal, Willie went to the city to get a guardrail put up in front of the house. They would not do it because they only allowed that on dead-end streets. So, he found some telephone poles, went out, and cut them so he could place them in

LESSON 6

the ground in front of our house. His nephew Herman Dixon helped him dig the holes and put them in the ground. He wanted to make sure that if something like that ever happened again, the car would be stopped by the poles. We never had any other crashes happen after that.

♥ ♥ ♥ ♥

LESSON 7

TO LIVE A LONG LIFE, GROW YOUR OWN FOOD AND STAY ACTIVE

WILLIE'S WISDOM

When I was growing up, my dad had a small farm. As I mentioned earlier, he grew a variety of vegetables. So, it was only natural that I would do some gardening when I became an adult. When I was working, I did not have time to do it, but once I retired, it became a routine pastime for me to plant crops year around.

My father taught me that it is best to plant summer crops beginning around April 1st. You can plant tomatoes, peas, corn, beans, watermelon, cucumbers, sugar cane, or okra. In the fall, around September, it is best to plant collards, turnips, and cabbage.

Sometimes the greens, collards, and turnips will turn yellow if they are not getting enough rain. When this happens, you take off the bottom leaves that have parched up. You can use fertilizer soda and put it down on the rows. It melts into the soil when it rains, and this causes the crop to turn green again. My dad used this method in his garden, and I still use it to this day.

Planting Process

When I get ready to plant the garden, I break the soil up with a hoe and shovel. I used to have a tiller, but it broke, and I did not replace it. I make my rows with the hoe and make sure they are about a foot apart, so there is space to walk down between

LESSON 7

them. If I have plants, I just dig holes with my garden scooper and put the plant down in the hole. Then I put a little lime or fertilizer around the plant and pour water into the hole.

If I am planting seeds, I make the rows up the same by using the hoe to open up the ground a little bit. Then, I put the seeds down into the holes. I also put down lime and fertilizer and more lime. I use my rake to put dirt over the seeds. The seeds start to come up in about seven to eight days. I do not put water in the hole with the seeds because I just wait for the rain. Rainwater is better for the crop. After the seeds come up, I use the hoe to put dirt around them so they will continue to grow, and this supports the plant so it will not blow over. I continue to check on the crops from there.

Gardening Tips:

Best Items for Winter — Collards, turnips, and cabbage, because insects and worms are not out in the cold, so this allows your crops to grow insect-free.

Best Items for Summer — Tomatoes, peas, corn, butter beans, and cucumbers. The worms sometimes get into tomato plants, so keep an eye out for this.

Hardest Crops to Grow — Corn and peas are hard to get to come up because you have to plant the seeds. Corn is the most difficult, but once you get them to come up, they stay up just fine.

Buy a half-pound of dry pea seeds. Put them in the freezer, even though they are already hard. Keep them in the freezer for a couple of weeks. Make rows in your garden and add fertilizer. Take your seeds from the freezer and plant them. This works well because the seeds will go into soil that is at room temperature, and being frozen helps them burst into the ground and open sooner. The peas will come up in about five days after being planted. The corn takes about seven days.

Easiest Things to Grow — Instead of seeds, get plants that have sprouted and are ready to be planted. You can use any kind of greens. Make sure to water them every day for three to four days in the evening when the sun goes down. The greens will catch root and grow on their own. After about six or seven days, you will want to put a little dirt around them.

Collards, Turnips, and Cabbage — Use a sack of miracle-gro potting soil and lime in the rows of your garden, and then plant the crops. In two weeks, you will want to use a hoe to carve out the rows. You can also use miracle-grow powder and mix it with water to make a solution you can sprinkle on each plant every three weeks.

Fill the holes with dirt. I place about twelve plants in each row. Collards take about two and a half months. I do not plant collards in the summer because they do not like the weather. Worms and bugs get to them and eat the leaves. In the winter, you won't have to worry about that, so it is best to grow these in the winter, along with cabbage and turnips. The cold weather is good for the greens.

The heat makes collard plants tough, so they are not as good in the summer. Seeds for collard greens take too long to grow, so plants are always better. I usually have four rows of collards. I use fertilizer and lime to help them start growing. After three weeks or so, I use miracle-gro plant food and spray them down. I do this every eight to ten days. This helps them grow big and stay green. They also need the right smart amount of water. Just remember that too much water can make them turn yellow.

Peas — You need to dig up the soil, make the rows, loosen the soil, plant the seeds, add water, and then cover them up. Add fertilizer and lime to the garden rows. It takes about seven days before you will see any growth. Then you will want to use the hoe to rake around them. After about six weeks, add more fertilizer and water. It takes about three months from planting to harvesting. I use seeds for peas and corn.

Fruit Trees — I have one apple tree that Jessie brought from Butler. We planted it, and it just grew. The problem here is that the birds peck at them, as well as the squirrels. You can get various fruit trees, such as orange, fig, and peach trees. Sometimes it is a hit or miss with our apple tree. It blooms each year, and sometimes we get lots of apples. Other times, there are fewer. If you decide to get a tree, you will just have to wait and see how it takes.

Pecan Tree — We had a pecan tree that just came up in our backyard. I did not plant it and do not know how it came to be; it just appeared one day. For years, we had pecans. It was a great tree because I did not have to do anything to maintain it. Pecans would just grow from year to year. The problem again here was that the squirrels would get into the pecans and knock them off the trees before they were ready.

The good thing here is that the squirrels did not eat crops out of the gardens, so there was no problem there. On occasion, rabbits would get into the garden, and birds would eat the peas. So, these crops have to be picked regularly whenever they are ready.

Time for Growth:

Cabbage — twelve weeks

Collards — ten weeks

Corn — three months

Cucumbers — six to seven weeks (These are *fast-growing*.)

Peas — three months (We would have enough peas to last us through the winter.)

Peppers — two and a half to three months (Plant these in either a pot or in the ground.)

Sugar Cane — Buy a stalk of cane from the fruit stand and bury it in the ground, and it will come up. That usually happens in the spring if you cut it all the way down to the ground in October. It will sprout during the first part of April.

Tomatoes – ten weeks, use plants

Turnips – eight weeks (Once the seeds are in the ground, it takes about three to four days to grow.)

We freeze the collards and peas and eat them every week. Once they freeze, we just take them out to cook, and they are just as fresh as when we first put them in.

While I prefer to have my garden in the ground in my yard, there are ways for you to have a garden if you do not have access

LESSON 7

to this. You can use pots, hanging baskets, and a tower garden, and I have even seen some people make a garden out of wood pallets. Just decide what you want to plant, determine if it is possible to grow what you want, and go from there. Gardening is enjoyable and relaxing, and it gives you homegrown food that you can be proud of.

♥ ♥ ♥ ♥

JESSIE'S JEWELS

Farming was a way of life for our family growing up as well. I developed a love for gardening and growing flowers. It became a hobby of mine, and I have always had some type of flower growing in every place I have lived. I love flowers, especially the red verbena flower. My mother grew those flowers when I was little, and I always remember them.

I guess you can say I have a green thumb. I have been successful in growing various plants and flowers, such as hibiscus, ferns, gardenias, and marigolds. It is very calming and relaxing to work with the plants. I make sure I water and feed them regularly.

Sometimes when it rains, I like to set my flowers and plants out to absorb the rainwater because it seems to help them grow stronger. Rainwater has better nutrients and makes them stay green. Sometimes I talk to the plants like people talk to their animals. When I talk to the plants, it certainly makes a difference (whether you know it or not) because they perk up and seem livelier.

♥ ♥ ♥ ♥

Willie posing by his collards for the season.

Cabbage from Willie Sr.'s garden.

Cabbage and collards in Willie Sr.'s garden.

Corn in Willie Sr.'s garden.

Peas growing in the garden.

Tomatoes growing in the garden. Sometimes eaten green and other times red when ripe.

Willie Sr., tending to his garden.

LESSON 8

NO MATTER THE AGE, IF YOU HAVE THE DESIRE AND ABILITY TO TRAVEL, THEN GO

WILLIE'S WISDOM

As a child, we rarely traveled. We visited my grandparents, who lived nearby, and took one trip to Theodore, as I recall. I did not go to Mobile until I moved there as an adult. My first family vacation was to Atlanta when we went with our good friends, Levi and Sarah Horne, in 1977. We went to Six Flags Amusement Park and Stone Mountain in Georgia. Other than that, the only travel I did was to visit my parents and Jessie's hometown in Butler. I had never been on an airplane until I started winning trips from the bus rodeo.

Prior to my retirement, we would visit our son Willie Jr., his wife, Dorothy, and their daughters Dominque and Sydney in Orlando. We also visited Angela in Houston. We even ventured out on our own in 2010 and took a Carnival Cruise.

The port was right in our city, so it just made sense for us to start there. Angela arranged everything for us, and it was the best vacation I had ever been on up until that time. The ship had entertainment, excursions, and all the food you could eat. We met a nice family on the ship and took a tour of Cozumel with them. We went on the cruise ship again in 2018 with Jessie's family.

One of the places I always wanted to go to was Hawaii. Well, that dream came true in 2015. Our daughter Angela took us to Honolulu, Hawaii. I had seen Hawaii on television, and it looked like a beautiful place. I wondered if it would look the same in person. I never imagined I would go there, but we did.

It took us eight hours on the flight from Houston to travel there. The length was not as bad as I thought it would be. I got up and walked around every hour or so, and before I knew it, we were there. We stayed in the Hilton Hawaiian Village on Waikiki Beach. Just a few steps from our hotel room, and we were on the sand. The water was right there.

One day, I walked down to the edge of the water and put my feet in, and just stared off into the distance. After all those years of wondering if Hawaii would look as beautiful as it did on television, I could see then that it was. We stayed there for a week. Angela and I would get up and go for walks along the boardwalk. They had fireworks at night and a live band playing on the beach. We took a tour around the island and even went to a pineapple farm. We made fresh Hawaiian leis and went to a luau where they roasted a pig in the ground and provided all sorts of different native cuisine. I even got in the pool, and that was a lot of fun. When Angela asked us where else we wanted to go, I mentioned New York City. Jessie suggested Washington, D.C., or Las Vegas. From that year on, Angela would take us on a trip every year.

In 2016, we went to Washington, D.C. We visited notable sites in the city like the White House and the Dr. Martin Luther King Jr. Memorial. We toured the U.S. Capital and the new National Museum of African American History and Culture that had just opened the weekend before our arrival.

On that trip, we were joined by Wilbur and Juliet Warfield, friends of Angela from her time working for the U.S. Army in Pennsylvania.

Amtrak was our mode of transportation in 2018 when we visited New York City. That was our first time on a train. It took about thirty-two hours, but it was an enjoyable ride to go along and see the countryside. We traveled through many states, including Mississippi, Alabama, Georgia, South Carolina, North Carolina, Virginia, Maryland, Delaware, Pennsylvania, and New Jersey. In New York, we toured the city and visited the Statue of Liberty. I went up inside, up to the pedestal, and looked out over the harbor. We also went to the famous Apollo Theater's amateur night. We had great seats on the floor up close and enjoyed the experience. We ate at a very popular restaurant in Harlem called Sylvia's.

In 2019, we went to Las Vegas and the Grand Canyon. I had quite a time touring the strip and downtown Vegas. We went for my 81st birthday. Angela arranged for us to have VIP, front-row seats at the Hitzville Motown review show, and then we had dinner at the Rainforest Cafe. The performers at the review even wished me a happy birthday. The Las Vegas strip was a sight to see it all lit up at night. We stayed at a Hilton property and also enjoyed a day by the pool.

We drove to Arizona and spent two days at Grand Canyon National Park. Seeing the mountains and hills and how the road zigs and zags through the countryside was something else. And the Grand Canyon was grand indeed. We were able to get a senior pass for twenty dollars for our car. It could be used in any

LESSON 8

U.S. National Park for an entire year. On the way back to Las Vegas, we stopped at the Hoover Dam, another U.S. landmark.

So, while I did not travel a lot while raising a family, I have made up for it in the subsequent years by being able to travel and see places I have only dreamed about. If you maintain your health and spirit, I believe the possibilities are endless. We had plans for other trips, but with the declaration of a global pandemic in 2020, we decided it was better to stay safe at home during that time. We did venture out in the summer of 2021 for Angela's 50th birthday. Jessie will share more on that, but just know that I had the time of my life.

♥ ♥ ♥ ♥

JESSIE'S JEWELS

Like Willie, my family never really traveled when I was growing up. We only visited my grandparents, who lived up the road in Jachin, Alabama, and other relatives in the area. The first time I went on an actual trip was when I was a cheerleader in the seventh and eighth grades. We went to nearby towns like Silas and Millry for the basketball games. Then when I was in high school, I would travel to Birmingham to visit my uncles and aunts in the summer.

The first trip that was of some distance that I recall was one we took with our friends, the Horne family, as Willie mentioned.

We drove a camper to Atlanta and stayed in a Western Inn Hotel. We later went on some trips with our church, Mt. Olive Baptist Church, #2. I took Angela and Willie Jr. on a trip with my sister-in-law Bonnie's church to Disney World in the early 1980s. Willie Sr. did not go because he was not able to take off work.

Of course, the first time I was on a plane, was when Willie won the bus rodeos. The first trip was to Los Angeles, California, in 1985. He mentioned all the other places that we went to, and they were all so nice. I truly enjoyed visiting Montreal, Canada. The city was so nice and very clean. All the trips were great, and it was just fun to be able to visit other cities. The bus rodeo events were fun because they would always have so many activities. They would even have celebrity impersonators perform. You could hardly tell that they were not the real person; they looked so much like them.

We always enjoyed our visits to see Willie Jr. and his family, and Angela, in the various cities they have lived in over the years. Such visits took us to Orlando, Florida, Chambersburg, Pennsylvania, Moline, Illinois, Iowa City, Iowa, and Houston, Texas. Willie mentioned the trips Angela has taken us on. The last trip we had with Willie Jr. was in June 2018, when we went on a family reunion Carnival Cruise to Mexico.

We had a great time. It was good to see everyone enjoying themselves. My sister Bessie Mae went on the trip with us. That was her first time going on a vacation like that and her first time on a cruise. Her daughters Cynthia, Carolyn, Ann, and Teina also joined in, along with my nieces Shirley, Cathy, Shalonda, Sherrita, Lauren, and Shante, as well as my nephews, Terrell and Brandon. I tried to get my other sisters and brothers to go, but they said that the ocean was just too much water for them.

Another notable trip I remember was when Angela won an all-expenses-paid trip to the Ellen DeGeneres show in Los Angeles from a Houston television station KHOU. Angela has won a lot of trips to places like Las Vegas, Paris, Amsterdam, Washington, D.C., New Orleans, and several trips to Los Angeles. She is working on her own book to share all about how she has been able to win trips and so many other things. Angela has been on three of America's favorite game shows, Wheel of

Fortune, The Price is Right, and Let's Make a Deal; and won on all of them!

When she wins trips, she always asks Willie and me if we want to go, and we always say no, that she should take a relative or friend. Well, this time, when she asked if I wanted to go, I did not hesitate to say yes. People spent years trying to get tickets to the Ellen show, so I was not going to pass that up. It was a great time. We flew out there from Houston and stayed in a hotel near Warner Brothers studios. We had VIP passes, and they gave us a gift bag filled with Ellen items like shirts, mugs, hats, and even Ellen underwear. We visited some popular eateries in the area and ended our trip with tickets to the Price is Right. I was not selected to come on down, but our family member Terlisa Sheppard who'd come along with us, was chosen and got to go up on stage. This made the trip all the better. We had on matching shirts, too, and I am sure that got the producer's attention.

One of my all-time favorite trips was to the Oprah Winfrey and Gayle King Girlfriend Getaway Cruise on Holland American Cruise Line, in January 2019. It was a Christmas and birthday present from Angela. We went on a new ship named the Nieuw Statendam. The cruise went to a private island in Half Moon Cay in the Bahamas.

We had a room with a balcony that was very nice. We heard Oprah speak, and since we sat in the fourth row of the arena, we were very close to the stage. We sat next to Pat Smith, who was the wife of NFL player Emmitt Smith. She was so lovely, and she took a picture with us. I also met Gayle King while on the beach in the Bahamas. She was very nice and personable.

LESSON 8

The vacation was so nice; the food, entertainment, and activities, were all some of the best. Angela's friend Tamika and her mother Pam went on the cruise as well, so we had a good time hanging out with them.

In 2020, the coronavirus pandemic hit, which put a stop to all of our trips. It took some getting used to being home all the time and not being able to go anywhere, but we had to do that to be safe. We traveled during the pandemic in May 2020 after Willie Jr. passed away to attend his service in Houston. We are thankful to my niece Shirley, her husband Terrell, and her daughter Shalonda for bringing us to the service. It was right in the middle of the pandemic, and so many people were getting sick, so for them to take us was a blessing. It was a very sad time, but it was good to be around the family with Willie Jr.'s wife Dorothy and daughters, Dominique and Sydney, during that time.

We did not travel anywhere again until August 2021. Angela turned fifty and planned a small private getaway just for ten of us family members. While she wanted to celebrate her birthday, she wanted to make sure everyone stayed safe. She only invited a few family members. Mainly, those who had been most helpful to Willie and me after our son passed away.

It was a chance to celebrate Angela's birthday and also to thank them for their love and support during those difficult times. We went to Anna Maria Island, Florida. I had never heard of it, but Angela learned of the island from one of her online business law students. The student was from there and recommended it as a nice place to visit. She was certainly right.

The island was about seven miles long. We had a rental house just steps from the white, sandy beach. The weather was great the entire time. There were some great restaurants there too, and the people were so friendly.

We were joined on that trip by James and Addie Patton, Brent and Felicia Poellnitz, Terlisa and Alyah Sheppard, and Felica Turner. Angela had a theme for each day, like a '70s night, game night, pool party, etc. We took a private boat tour on the water and saw the dolphins. We ate at a nice restaurant on the beach called the Sandbar for her birthday.

The mode of transportation was primarily golf carts, so Angela rented one. We rode around the island, sightseeing and enjoying the area. It was one of the best vacations. We all were happy to go somewhere, and it was so nice to be with family members sharing good food and having fun. I made sure to wear the shirt with Willie Jr.'s picture on it that my daughter-in-law Felicia made for me, just to make sure he was there with us.

In May 2022, we traveled to Nashville, Tennessee, to see our granddaughter, Dominique, graduate from Meharry Medical College. It was wonderful to see her reach her goal, knowing how much she has experienced over these last few years. I know our son, Willie Jr., was beaming down from the heavens.

Our most recent trip was to celebrate Willie Sr. turning 85 years old in May. Angela surprised us with a trip to New Orleans for a few days. We still are cautious about venturing out so she was able to ask our cousin Devon Hodges if we could stay at his Airbnb. My cousin has his own tropical oasis. I was amazed at all the flowers and greenery he had. It was so nice and peaceful,

LESSON 8

and we spent hours sitting outside under the canopies and I enjoyed looking at his many plants and flowers. On Willie's birthday, we were joined by Brent and Felicia, and we went on the Natchez Steamboat for a jazz lunch cruise. The weather was perfect, and we had a great lunch complete with catfish, red beans and rice, potato salad, jambalaya and some delicious bread pudding. After the lunch cruise, we relaxed lounging by the pool enjoying the breeze and the company. Sometimes you do not have to go far to have a great adventure, it may be just down the road a bit.

We have had some great travels, but we are not done. As long as we are in good health and it is safe to travel, we plan to enjoy more places. I definitely want to go to Chicago when the Obama Presidential Center is complete. That would also give me a chance to visit my aunt Frankie, uncle William, and cousin Terry.

So, if you have the desire to travel, make it happen. A whole world beyond where you live awaits you. Go and explore it.

♥ ♥ ♥ ♥

Willie Sr., Willie Jr. and Angela on the first trip to Atlanta, Georgia

Celebrating Willie Sr's 85th birthday in New Orleans

Willie, Sr. and Jessie on their first carnival cruise to Mexico.

Jessie, Angela, Willie, Sr. and Felica in Las Vegas for Willie's 81st birthday. This was Willie and Jessie's first time in Las Vegas.

Willie Sr. and Jessie at the Grand Canyon

Willie Sr., taking in the sites at the Hoover Dam in Nevada.

Jessie's family reunion cruise to Mexico.

Willie Sr., Jessie, Angela, Shalonda, Terrell and Shirley on the Coleman family reunion cruise to Mexico.

Willie Sr. and Jessie in New York City at the Statute of Liberty.

Jessie and Willie Sr. in Honolulu, Hawaii at the Hilton Hawaiian Village on Waikiki Beach.

Jessie at the Price is Right in Los Angeles, California.

Robin Roberts, Jessie and Angela at Good Morning America in New York City.

Jessie at Good Morning America in New York with host Michael Strahan.

Jessie with Gayle King in Half Moon Cay, Bahamas on the Oprah Winfrey and Gayle King Girlfriends Getaway Cruise.

Willie Sr. at the beach on Anna Maria Island, Florida celebrating Angela's 50th birthday.

Willie Sr. walking out into the ocean on Waikiki Beach in Hawaii

Willie Sr., Angela and Jessie at Madame Tussauds in Washington, D.C.

Jessie and Willie Sr. enjoying Honolulu, Hawaii.

Terlisa, Alyah, Addie, Jimmie, Jessie, Angela, Willie Sr., Felica, Felicia and Brent at Anna Maria Island, Florida for Angela's 50th birthday bash.

Visiting Madame Tussauds in Washington DC.

LESSON 9

YOU MAY NOT BE READY FOR LEADERSHIP, BUT SOMETIMES IT IS READY FOR YOU

WILLIE'S WISDOM

In the early 1970s, I was eligible to join the union at my job. Once you had worked ninety days, you could join. I was content just going to the meetings and listening to what was going on for many years. We would have union meetings once a month, and I would always attend. Many times, I would be asked to talk to other workers about joining the union. We would coach employees about what the benefits of membership were and all it had to offer.

In 1990, a lot of members asked me to put my name in the hat to be the vice president of the union. After I thought about it, I agreed to run for the position. I was elected and served a four-year term. My duties included reviewing write-ups of employees and sitting in on meetings if a member had been called in for issues or incidents on the job. I would advise them and give information on the disciplinary process. Serving as the vice president was a lot of responsibility. It paid a little money, and I would rather work and make money and do overtime, but I felt it was important to serve. Most times, I had to go to union obligations, so I could not work overtime. While it was a lot of work, I was glad that I could contribute, help, and advocate for my co-workers. Sometimes you are the best person for the role, and you just have to believe in yourself and know that you can serve and do the work.

LESSON 9

Another volunteer effort I was involved in was the neighborhood watch. We wanted to make sure the neighborhood was safe, so we would patrol the area to make sure everything was good. I did it for a couple of years. I was assigned a walkie-talkie so I could communicate with the other person patrolling that day. I would drive around the neighborhood for a couple of hours. During my time, I thankfully never had anything to report, but it was good to be able to contribute and give back to the community.

♥ ♥ ♥ ♥

JESSIE'S JEWELS

I served the community by being a part of the voting process. I started working at the voting polls in 1987. A man named Mr. Hogan was an inspector of poll workers, and he wanted to get more black people involved and working at the polls. My neighbor Jackie also decided to work with me. We initially worked at several locations but were finally located at the Boys' Club in our neighborhood.

I enjoyed meeting the other volunteers and people in the neighborhood and even served as the chief clerk for four years. The chief clerk had greater responsibilities, such as overseeing the absentee ballot counting process, keeping things in order, and doing additional paperwork. It was a lot of responsibility, but once I got used to it, it was fine. I truly enjoyed working at the polls.

When I first started, I made seventy-five dollars a day. It was not a lot of money, but it was good to be able to serve. I worked for twenty-five years, including the primaries and general elections. The last election I worked for was in 2012. The four years before that were an exciting time because President Barack Obama was elected.

We had a lot of people vote in the presidential election that year. It was even more exciting for me after the election because I went to the inauguration in Washington, D.C., My daughter

LESSON 9

Angela has a close friend Bridget Obikoya who lives there, and she had room for us to come and stay with her and her family. It was freezing cold during that year, but I wanted to be there and witness history. We were far in the back by the Washington Monument, but we could hear everything, and they had monitors, so it was wonderful being out there in all the excitement. There were no incidents, and everything went over smoothly.

For many years, I helped at our church's clothing and food pantry. We would organize clothes and food for those who were in need. We would then have days when people could come and get items from the pantry. We helped them and assisted with handing out what was needed.

I also served the community by answering the call for jury duty. I have served on juries several times. One time I was on a jury, and the discussion among the jurors became very heated. They were arguing over the case and could not reach an agreement.

It was an assault case where one man jumped on another and beat him up. The victim's father came and shot the man who was on trial. We deliberated, and three of us wanted to convict the guy, and the rest of the jury did not. We deliberated for days, and finally, three of us moved to the other side. The judge said he would not settle for a hung jury. The man was acquitted, and three days later, he went and killed the guy who shot him.

Serving will give you purpose and meaning. We set an example for our children, and they followed this path of service in many ways. We are proud of the fact that we raised them to serve freely and expect nothing in return.

LESSON 10

LIFE IS FULL OF CHALLENGES; DON'T BE AFRAID. HAVE FAITH, TAKE THEM ON, AND OVERCOME THEM

WILLIE'S WISDOM

Health challenges come and go. I have dealt with some of my own. In 2004, I was diagnosed with prostate cancer. I chose to have surgery to remove my prostate, and it was successful. Since that time, I have gone to my routine doctor visits and made sure my PSA levels are maintained. I am cancer-free, so I continue to thank the Lord for that. Being diagnosed was a scary time, but with the support of Jessie and the children, I made it through just fine.

I used to sit down driving the bus all day, so that did not lend itself to getting much exercise. I had gained weight and had high blood pressure, so Jessie and I started walking. After retiring, we would walk up to the grocery in the Crichton area for exercise.

We are not able to do that much walking now. We used to walk every day before daylight. I even walked all the way downtown. One day I was crossing the railroad tracks, and someone hollered at me, asking for something. He started chasing me, and I started walking faster. Then, I started running. He finally stopped, and I came on home. That made me more cautious about walking long distances. It took me an hour to walk downtown, then turn around, and return. Sometimes I would take the bus back.

LESSON 10

One of the main ways now that I stay active is to do yard work and wash my cars. I always maintained my own yard and still do to this day. I have a riding mower and a push mower. We have lots of greenery, trees, bushes, and flowers that I have maintained over the years. Working out in the yard gives me good exercise and fresh air. I always find things to do around the house, like edging, raking, and mowing. I even do a little painting from time to time.

I mentioned my first car early on. The second car I bought was a white 1978 Oldsmobile. I had it only a short time (about a year) because something went wrong with the motor. I followed that with a black Chevrolet Impala. I kept that car for quite a long time. I had a yellow Buick Skylark, a burgundy Oldsmobile Cutlass, a gray Mercury Cougar, and then an SUV.

I always kept my cars in pristine condition. They were always clean and looked like they had just come off the showroom floor. Some people said I should have started a car-detailing business, but I spend so much time on one car that I doubt I could make much money. So, I just enjoy making sure *my* cars are clean. I have been doing this for many years. As I mentioned earlier, when I lived with my brother W.L., I kept his cars clean too, and that was back in the late 1960s. It is just something I have always enjoyed. I get compliments on my vehicles all the time, and I take pride in having them look so good.

♥ ♥ ♥ ♥

JESSIE'S JEWELS

Maintaining good health is very important. One of the ways to do this is to cook meals at home. Since we grow a lot of our own food, it is easy to eat healthily. I try to always cook with nutritious oils, seasonings, fresh garlic, onions, and other ingredients that add flavor, but not too much salt.

One of my favorite breakfast meals to make is salmon patties, grits, and biscuits. I usually make this on Sundays. One of my favorite dinners is red beans and rice and Conecuh sausages with cornbread. I also make smothered pork chops, rice, black eye peas, gumbo, fried chicken, greens and more.

On Fridays, we typically have fried catfish with salad. I make traditional holiday meals with turkey or ham, cornbread dressing, macaroni and cheese, potato salad, collard greens, and of course, sweet tea (a staple in the South). I prepared many southern dishes that I learned to cook from watching my mother when I was growing up. This has served me well and ensures that we always have the right mixture of meats and vegetables to maintain a good diet.

We have excellent medical providers and always make sure to have our yearly examinations and appointments. One of the challenges I had years ago was a thyroid issue. I was in my fifties. The doctors realized it was the thyroid, and it had to be

LESSON 10

removed. A few years ago, I had surgery for an ulcer, and I spent a few days in the hospital. As you age, you experience typical things like high blood pressure, arthritis, etc., but we take it in stride and stay active.

We have been members of Greater Mount Olive Baptist Church #2, where the Reverend Hubert Baker has been the pastor for many years. It is wonderful to have a great home church where you can worship and fellowship. This has been a source of strength in the tough times that we all face in life, from health challenges to losing loved ones. The members of the church are family, and we celebrate and support each other. We share in the things that our children and family are doing. They always made us feel special when Angela was on her television game shows. They would announce such milestones in church and encourage everyone to watch.

♥ ♥ ♥ ♥

LESSON 11

WHEREVER YOU MAY GO OR LIVE, FIND THE JOY THE CITY HAS TO OFFER

WILLIE & JESSIE

We came to Mobile for a better life. As we told you earlier, growing up in the country, there were a lot of things we did not have. Mobile provided progress and stability for us. It has been over sixty-six years, and for Jessie, sixty years. While some people may complain about Mobile and say that it is slow and there is not much to do, they are just not making the most of what it has to offer.

Our daughter Angela asked us about the Civil Rights era and how it was in Mobile during that time. Most of the big events happened in cities like Birmingham, Montgomery, and Selma. Although Mobile had marches, we did not participate in them, but we supported those who did. There were notable individuals like John L. LeFlore, an activist, and leader in the National Association for the Advancement of Colored People, who made a big impact on the civil rights movement in Mobile. The high school Willie Jr. and Angela went to is named after Mr. LeFlore.

Mobile has a little bit of everything—parks, museums, shopping, minor league sports, movie theaters, and of course, our claim to fame—the Mobile Mardi Gras. Mobile is the birthplace of Mardi Gras, which was started back around 1703 by French explorers. The city is very proud of this. Mardi Gras is

LESSON 11

an annual celebration of parades, balls, parties, and revelry that goes on for two weeks before coming to an end on Fat Tuesday, the day before Lent begins.

At the parades, float riders throw everything—beads, cups, coins, stuffed animals, and even MoonPies (the famous graham cracker and marshmallow-filled snack cake). Some have been known to pass little bottles of liquor to revelers. It is a time to get together with family and friends and celebrate. When the children were growing up, we used to take them downtown to the Mardi Gras parades. We would load up the car, park near Washington Avenue, and listen to music on the radio while we waited for the parade to go by.

Willie Jr. and Angela always had a ball catching the trinkets. When they came home, they would spread everything on the floor and fight over who got what. They always settled on what the other liked the most. Of course, we did other things, like going to the mall and taking the children to Sunday school, where they would participate in the programs offered. We would sometimes take the children to go get pizza or McDonald's. During the Christmas holidays, we enjoyed taking the children on a drive down Siena Vista street, which was in a neighborhood not far from us. All of the neighbors there would decorate their houses with lots of lights, and it is always exciting to see and very popular to do in the city.

One of the best things about living in Mobile was being so close to our family. As adults, we lived within five to ten minutes of our siblings. We would make the rounds over to their houses on Sundays. The children loved going over to the relatives because that is where everyone would meet up. My sister Bonnie always had a house full of visitors. She would make a down-home Sunday meal complete with cakes. Her specialty was her famous pound cake.

Jessie's brother, B.C., lived down the street from my brother W.L., so we always visited them as well. I think this rings true for many families in Mobile, and it keeps everyone close-knit. We would also see our family back in Butler and Nicholsville/Dixon Mills. During the summers, Jessie and the children would take the Greyhound bus to go stay with her family for a week or two.

So, while Mobile might not have the bright lights of a big city, it has a down-home feel and is a nice place to raise a family. And now, it's a pleasant place to be retired.

♥ ♥ ♥ ♥

LESSON 12

ALWAYS REMEMBER THOSE WHO CAME BEFORE YOU AND THINK OF THOSE WHO WILL COME AFTER YOU

When you reach eighty-five and seventy-nine years old, you will have your share of loss. We have lost parents, siblings, cousins, and friends. But of course, nothing could have prepared us for the sudden loss of our son Willie Jr. Dealing with his sudden death on April 25, 2020, was like losing a part of our own body. I know we will never get over it, but we are learning to live with it. Willie Jr. was a great son, and we try to always remember the great times we had together. Here are some of our memories of him growing up, along with those of a few family members and friends who watched him grow up as well.

Childhood Memories of Willie Jr.
Willie Sr. and Jessie's Memories:
One day when it was raining out, and I was pregnant with Willie Jr., my neighbor hollered over to tell me because I had some clothes on the line. I ran out to try to get them and fell down the stairs of the house. It was about six concrete steps, and I was almost at the end. I had my house shoes on, and I slipped and fell. All that day and the next day, Junior did not move. The day after that, I was going to go to the doctor, and just before I was about to leave, he started moving around again. I was so relieved.

Willie Jr. took his first trip when he was three months old. His grandmother, Mamie wanted to see him, and my sister-in-law Bonnie was going to visit them, so she took him with her. She was just going for the day. They were supposed to return by 4:00 p.m. but did not return. We were so worried. They did

LESSON 12

not return until 1:00 a.m. because the car broke down on the highway. We were glad when they finally came back, and all was well.

Sometimes I would take the bus, and Willie Jr., and I would go downtown for a few hours. Usually, we would end up at Woolworths because he liked to eat at the counter. I would buy him a toy, and then we would take the bus and come on back home. It was not far, but he always enjoyed being on the bus and looking out the window.

Willie Jr.'s first job was selling newspapers for the Mobile Press-Register when he was fourteen. He wanted a job to have some spending money for school and activities. He would sell the newspapers on the weekends at a little store in Toulminville on Stanton Road.

One day, he went inside to get some snacks and left his money outside. We have no idea why he would do that, but he was in there just a little while, and when he came back, all of his money was gone. That was the last day he sold papers.

One afternoon, Willie Jr. was coming from the Boys' Club around the corner. He was supposed to be back before dark. It was raining out, and he saw a car barreling toward him. He tried to step up on the curb to avoid it, missed it, and fell to the ground.

One of his friends, Michael, was with him and came and told us that he had fallen and hurt himself. When we went outside, he was on the ground, and when we got him to the hospital, we realized he had broken his leg. They had to cut off his new jeans to put on the cast, and of course, he was upset about that because they were his favorite pair. It was quite an ordeal for him. It was painful, but he healed just fine.

Willie Jr.'s first car was a brown Chevrolet Chevette. He was proud because he had saved his money for that car, and we helped as well. The car was a standard shift, so it was a challenge trying to get him to learn to drive it. It was nothing fancy, but it got him where he needed to go.

Angela's Memories:

I had some great times with my brother, from sharing the same room until I was probably about ten years old to wearing his band uniform that was way too big for me. I remember in elementary school, our cousin Toby (RIP) came over to our house to go to school with us. He usually came by early, around 6:00 a.m.

I would have to get out of my bed and go to Mom and Dad's room. I remember always whining and asking why I had to get up and leave my bed. Before I went to my parent's room, I would look over, and my brother would be sound asleep. Eventually, Junior and Toby would get up and get ready for school. I would hear them laughing and talking more than anything else. Toby did not have any siblings, so his cousins were the next best thing.

We had lots of fun times playing with the neighborhood children who would come over to our house. We had a swing and a fenced-in area where we skated and played games. One of our neighbors, Eugene Phillips, came over a lot, and I remember how he would always strike a pose when we took pictures. We always thought that was so funny.

LESSON 12

When my brother worked at the store, he would often bring me my favorite items. Sometimes, just out of kindness and other times, to bribe me to keep my mouth shut about any number of things. Let's just say I had my share of M&M's and Oreos for sure.

My brother and I were four years apart, so we were never at the same school until high school. I remember when I first started high school in the ninth grade, my brother was a senior. He had his group of friends, and sometimes they would call me Lil JD, as that was their nickname for him, just to tease me. Despite that, it was cool to know people in the twelfth grade. Of course, sometimes it was a pain to have my brother in the same school.

One day I was in the cafeteria, and this upperclassman was talking to me. All of a sudden, out of nowhere, I heard my brother say, "Man, what you doing talking to my sister?" He spoke in his stern voice while standing over us. The guy got up so fast, and he was gone, never daring to speak to me again. I thought oh boy, this is going to be a long year! It was a great time, though, because his friends always looked out for me that school year.

Uncle Lemoral Coleman's Memories:
Willie and I had a lot of fun riding bikes on the hot summer days when he would come to visit us in Butler with my sister Jessie Mae and niece, Angela. Willie and I would go fishing and camp out at my treehouse. Only a few people knew where it was. We enjoyed playing basketball, and I had a bicycle rim for

my goal. We would go picking corn and watermelon in the field, just having a great time. The good old days. We loved them.

Marlon Gover, Childhood Best Friend, Memories:

When we were in middle school, we went on a trip to Six Flags Amusement Park in Atlanta, Georgia. We went with the Boys' Club around the corner from our house. We took pictures throughout the park. When we came home and developed the pictures, JD (what we called Willie) realized his idol Charles Barkley was not only at the park but also in one of our pictures. JD would not allow himself to cuss, so he would substitute words like 'your butt' or 'your tail' for swear words. He was my boy.

Marcus Lewis, Classmate, Memories:

I remember going around with Willie when he filmed weddings and high school football games in Mobile for WALA FOX 10. When I worked in radio, he would call me during my overnight shift at the station, and we would talk for hours about various topics, from sports to the broadcasting industry. I worked from 12:00 a.m. to 6:00 a.m., and when I got home, I would fall asleep around 10:00 a.m.

Willie usually would call me during the middle of the day when I was sleeping to wake me up.

He would say, "Hey man, what you doing?"

I would tease him and say, "Just checking my eyelids for cracks."

A lot of times, we would ride to the mall on the weekends during our off days and hang out. We took classes together in the

LESSON 12

same department (Mass Communication) and graduated from Alabama State University in Montgomery together. We were in each other's weddings too. I remember when Dominique was a baby. He brought her to my wedding. They both danced to the Macarena song at my reception and had the best time. I even have that on tape.

Addie Patton, Cousin, Memories

From a little boy, Junior was always a sweet and polite kid. During his senior year, we talked a lot about life.

Norma Cromwell, Cousin, Memories

When Aunt Jessie and Uncle Willie traveled out of town, they would have me and my son Mario come and stay with Angela and Junior for a few days. Junior had to be about fifteen, but he was already six feet tall.

One evening, we all went to Popeye's to pick up dinner. After ordering, I attempted to pay.

Suddenly, I heard this big, booming voice say, "Put that back. I've got money!"

The look on the cashier's face was one of shock and pure sympathy.

I looked at him and politely said, "You don't talk to me like that. I'm the adult here, not you."

I do know he meant well, but the way it came out was something else. That became my fondest memory of Junior. It always made me laugh when I thought about it.

♥ ♥ ♥ ♥

STANTAN ROAD SCHOOL
1974-75

IN MEMORY OF
WILLIE DIXON

Marcus Lewis and Willie Jr. at their graduation from Alabama State University.

Friend Marlon Gover and Willie Jr.

LESSON 13

DON'T TAKE YOURSELF SO SERIOUSLY; MAKE SURE TO STOP AND SMELL THE ROSES. JUST HAVE FUN!

WILLIE'S WISDOM

When my daughter Angela was in college, she was a part of the debutante ball with the Athenian Social Club. This event is for presenting young ladies to society. We all had to dress up in tuxedos and present our daughters at the ball. I had never gone to an event like that before, but it was such a great time because we had food, beverages, and music. We all danced. Now I am not really one for dancing, but I cut a rug that night.

One day, I was visiting Houston and went over to Willie Jr.'s house. They had a scooter, and I took it for a spin. Angela asked me what I was doing, and I said, "having fun and feeling like I was a kid again." I had never been on a scooter, but it was so fun and made me remember the times I used to ride my bike with my brother W. L.

I was 80 when I had my first birthday party! When I was growing up, we did not have parties. My mother always made us cakes for our birthday, and we celebrated at home, but I never had a party, per se. When I turned 80, Angela organized a party at a local restaurant and invited some family and friends. We had my favorite foods: catfish, fries, hushpuppies, and slaw. The party had a western theme, so it was decorated with western items and trinkets. It was great to have all the family together,

LESSON 13

and friends join in. I was smiling once again like a kid and had the best time taking pictures with everyone and listening to the wonderful tributes everyone made.

Another good memory I have was finding $100. I was at McDonald's, and I looked down and thought it was play money. I picked it up and realized it was a real bill. It had rained that day, so it was wet, but once it had dried, it was as good as new. I gave it to my then-two-year-old granddaughter, Dominque.

♥ ♥ ♥ ♥

JESSIE'S JEWELS

People who know me always talk about how good my memory is and that I never forget anything. I guess it is a blessing to remember so much. I know sometimes people may question what I am saying but because they do not remember specifically like I do, they just keep it to themselves. If I am saying something, then it is facts. It still amazes me how much I remember sometimes.

I am also known for some favorite sayings. I use them for all types of situations, like when someone tells me good or bad news, when I am watching television, or just whenever the moment strikes me. Here are some of them:

"Good Lord from Zion!"

"Get on away from here!"

"Well, due Jesus!"

"Good Jesus!"

"So that's the way that is!"

"You big dummy!" (I said this while watching Wheel of Fortune when this black guy did not get the puzzle right. He really should have known that puzzle.)

A fun time for me was Angela's 50th birthday party. We had a 70's night, and everyone dressed in 70s attire. I did not have anything, so Angela gave me one of her outfits. We did a soul train line where we all paraded down in our outfits and then

LESSON 13

voted on who had the best strut and costume. Well, I won! I received a gift card to a restaurant and bragging rights!

Like Willie, I have a memory of finding money too. I found $200. I went to get a cart at the store, and there was a white envelope in the cart. Since there was no one around, I looked inside and discovered the money and kept it, and it really came in handy.

♥ ♥ ♥ ♥

WILLIE'S FAVORITE THINGS

- Favorite Colors: Red, white, and blue
- Favorite Foods: Peas, greens, fish, and chicken
- Favorite Places to Eat: Boiling Pot and the Golden Corral
- Favorite Flowers: Azaleas and roses
- Favorite Sports: Basketball and baseball
- Favorite Vacations: New York City and Anna Maria Island, Florida
- Favorite Cakes: German Chocolate Cake and Red Velvet Cake
- Favorite Cookies: Chocolate Chip and Oatmeal
- Favorite Drinks: Coca-Cola and Pepsi
- Favorite Song: "Joy Will Come" by the Mighty Clouds of Joy
- Favorite Decade: 1950s, taking cotton to the cotton gin at 4:00 a.m.
- Favorite Places to Shop: Walmart and JC Penny
- Favorite Candies: Milky Way and Baby Ruth
- Favorite Snacks: Potato chips and pork skins
- Favorite Thing You Did for Fun Growing Up: Bike riding
- Favorite Movies: All kinds of westerns, Driving Miss Daisy, and Radio

LESSON 13

- Favorite Holidays: <u>Thanksgiving and Christmas</u>
- Favorite TV Shows:<u> Wheel of Fortune and the Price is Right</u>
- Favorite Musical Artist: <u>James Brown</u>
- Favorite Book: <u>Comic Books</u>
- Favorite Outdoor Activity: <u>Growing my garden</u>
- Favorite Ice Cream: <u>Vanilla</u>
- Favorite Beverage: <u>Miller Lite</u>

♥ ♥ ♥ ♥

JESSIE'S FAVORITE THINGS

- Favorite Colors: <u>Blue and Green</u>
- Favorite Foods: <u>Fish and Chicken</u>
- Favorite Places to Eat: <u>Boiling Pot and the Golden Corral</u>
- Favorite Flower: <u>Any kind, all kinds, but especially the red Verbena</u>
- Favorite Sport: <u>Basketball</u>
- Favorite Vacations: <u>Hawaii and New York</u>
- Favorite Cakes: <u>Pound Cake and Sock It To Me Cake</u>
- Favorite Cookies: <u>Chocolate Chip Cookies and Vanilla Wafers</u>
- Favorite Drinks: <u>Coca-Cola and Sprite</u>
- Favorite Song: <u>Amazing Grace</u>
- Favorite Decades: <u>1950s and 1960s</u>
- Favorite Places to Shop: <u>Sears and Belk</u>
- Favorite Candy: <u>Butterfinger</u>
- Favorite Snacks: <u>Potato chips, cheese curls</u>
- Favorite Things You Did for Fun Growing Up: <u>Hopscotch and Jump Rope</u>
- Favorite Movie: <u>Driving Miss Daisy</u>
- Favorite Holidays: <u>Thanksgiving and Christmas</u>

LESSON 13

- Favorite TV Shows: <u>Good Times, The Jeffersons, The Cosby Show</u>
- Favorite Musical Artists: <u>The Temptations and Aretha Franklin</u>
- Favorite Book: <u>The Bible</u>
- Favorite Outdoor Activities: <u>Grilling and gardening</u>
- Favorite Ice Cream: <u>Vanilla and black walnut</u>
- Favorite Beverages: <u>Iced tea and lemonade</u>

♥ ♥ ♥ ♥

Willie Sr. at his 80th western themed birthday party. His first time having a party at 80!

Angela, Dorothy, Willie Sr., Willie Jr., Jessie and Brent at the 80th birthday party.

Willie Sr., and Minnie, sister-in-law at his 80th birthday party.

Friends Rev. Ronald and Gladys McCants, Jessie and Willie Sr. at his 80th birthday party.

Minnie, Bonnie, Willie Sr., Jessie and Annie Gray at his 80th birthday party.

Angela's debutante ball with Jessie, Willie Sr. Dorothy, Willie Jr. and escort Johnny Grandison Jr.

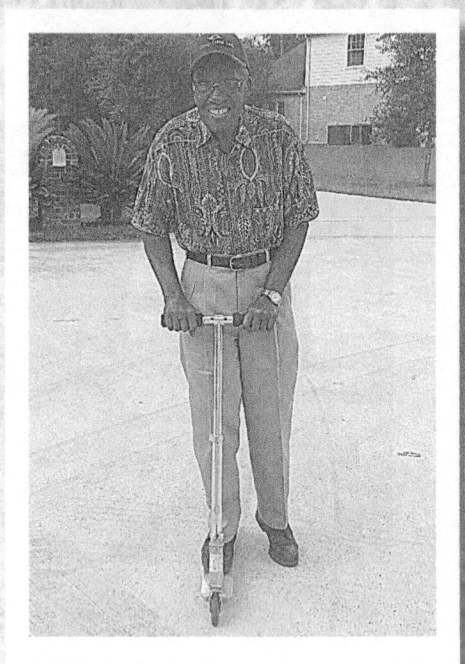

Willie Sr. having fun on the scooter while visiting Houston.

Willie Jr., Dorothy and granddaughter Sydney, Jessie, Willie Sr. and Angela at Sydney's National Charity League ball.

Willie Jr., Dorothy and granddaughters Dominique and Sydney

Tracie Melvin, Willie Sr., Jessie, Angela and Willie, Jr. at the University of Iowa College of Law graduation.

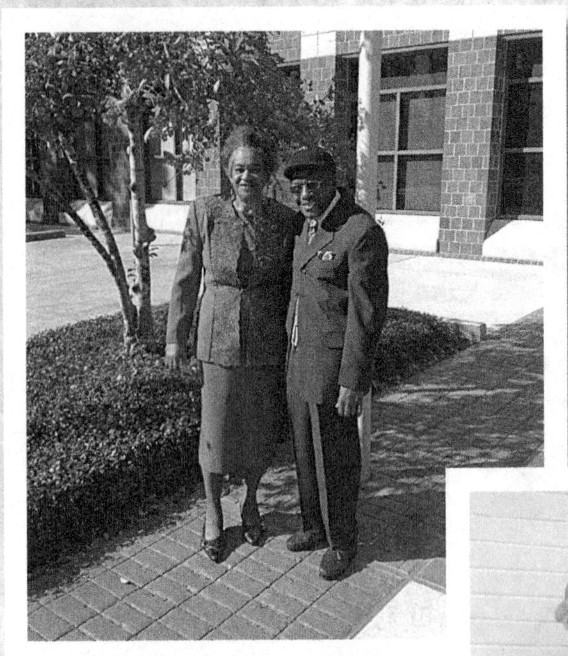

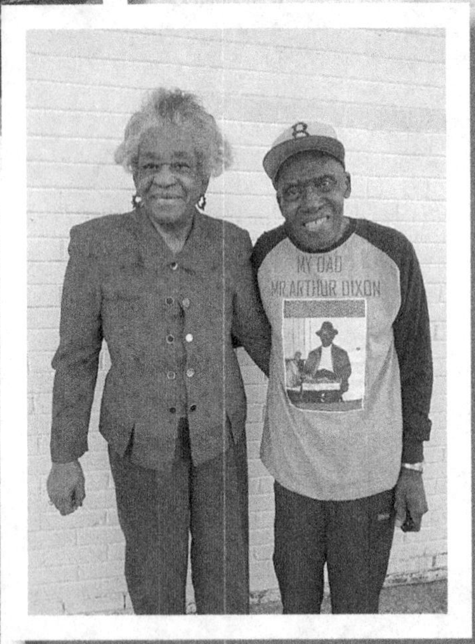
B
MY DAD
MR.ARTHUR DIXON

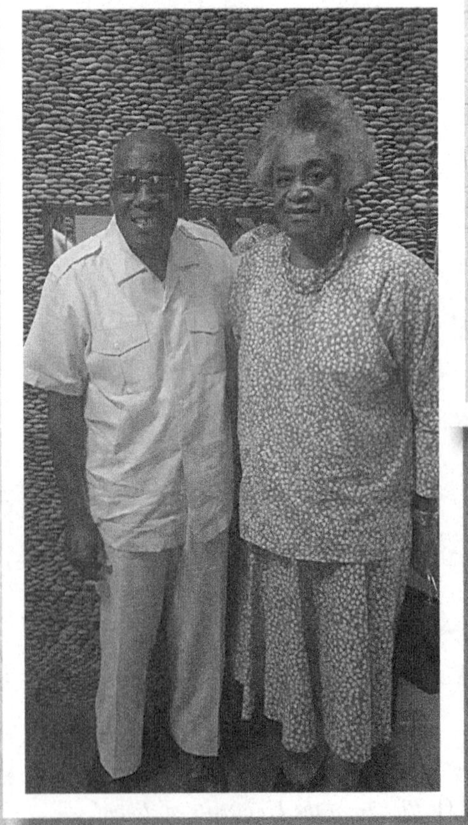

Happy Mardi Gras

FLASHBACK TO 1938

- U.S. President: Franklin D. Roosevelt
- Minimum wage: $.25/hour
- A gallon of gas: $.10
- New York Yankees won the World Series
- New York Giants won the NFL Championship
- #1 Song: *Begin the Beguine*, by Artie Shawn
- Movies Released: Bringing Up Baby, The Adventures of Robin Hood
- Cost of New Home – $3,900
- Average wages - $1,730
- Also born in 1938 – Shirley Caeser, Maxine Waters

FLASHBACK TO 1944

- U.S. President: Franklin D. Roosevelt
- Minimum wage: $.30/hour
- A gallon of gas: $.15
- St. Louis Cardinals won the World Series
- Green Bay Packers won the NFL Championship
- #1 Song: *Swinging on a Star*, by Bing Crosby
- Movies Released: Arsenic and Old Lace, Meet Me in St. Louis
- Cost of New Home - $3,450
- Average wages - $2,400
- Also born in 1944 – Diana Ross, Patti LaBelle, Gladys Knight and Sly Stone

LESSON 14

GIVE PEOPLE THEIR FLOWERS WHILE THEY CAN STILL SMELL THEM

ANGELA, Daughter

I added this lesson because I realized that there are many people, relatives, and friends that my dad and mom have impacted. I thought, wouldn't it be nice to include a chapter that highlights special moments and memories from family and friends? This is a surprise for Dad and Mom, so they will be reading these words when the book is published.

Thanks to everyone who contributed. We always say, "Give people their flowers while they can still smell them." Well, here is a wonderful aroma of love for all to enjoy!

There are so many things I can say about Mom and Dad. They always supported my brother and me in all that we wanted to do. They never tried to discourage us from stepping out and spreading our wings, and seeing what the world had to offer.

While they did not have the chance for higher education, they made sure that we did and told us we could be whatever we wanted to be. Our dreams came true thanks to their love, support, and funds, of course! It is a blessing to have parents who worked hard and saw the value of education.

As an adult, I am truly blessed to see them still enjoying the good life. It's the simple things, like visiting and watching them do their favorite things. Watching Dad wash the car and tend his garden. Watching Mom cook her famous red beans, rice, and gumbo, yet never helping (because I don't want to mess it up). I also enjoy just sitting on the back porch talking and laughing for hours, where I can ask countless questions about their childhood, my grandparents, how they met, and so on.

LESSON 14

Seeing them interact with each other sometimes is pure hilarity. I'm laughing just thinking about it.

I am glad that they continue to do things that they never imagined. We have traveled to many places, and it has been a joy to have those adventures. So, thanks, Dad and Mom, for being who you are and giving all you could to ensure our lives would be full and rich. You both are very different but fit together like a special-made puzzle. And for that, I am thankful.

Angela, daughter

♥ ♥ ♥ ♥

My fondest memories of my niece Jessie while growing up in Alabama were her visits to her grandparents, Lloyd and Minnie Hodges. Enjoying my mother Minnie's teacakes was a real treat. We would take long walks while admiring the beauty of the country wildflowers. We would share our goals of getting married and having a family of our own. We both fulfilled our dream of getting married after graduating high school. She married a very handsome man, Willie Dixon, Sr., and moved to Mobile, AL, while I married my husband William, and moved to Chicago, IL.

Jessie, although we are far away, I thank you for the close bond we share, even to this day. Your phone calls are always a blessing to me. I appreciate and love you dearly.

Frankie Cornelius, aunt

♥ ♥ ♥ ♥

My sweet memory of my sister Jessie is from when we were little girls. Papa built us a playhouse. We would help mom in the morning after breakfast and wash dishes. Then, we would take leftover biscuits, meat, kool-aid, our play tea set, and dolls to the playhouse. We would spread the dishes out, place food on them, pour kool-aid in the teacups, and then dress our dolls. At that time, our sisters Shirley, Minnie, and Bernice hadn't been born. So, this was one of my fondest memories of just the two of us together.

Bessie Johnson, sister

♥ ♥ ♥ ♥

Once when Papa got hurt, Jessie Mae came home, and Willie drove from Mobile to pick her up. We decided to hide her in the room. When Willie asked where she was, we told him she was gone. He started saying, "No! She's here," and kept repeating it. Finally, she came out, and they had a great laugh about it.

Shirley Ann Townsend, sister

♥ ♥ ♥ ♥

I remember whenever Willie and Jessie would visit, they had to have my fried chicken and mac and cheese. They knew that anytime they visited, I would always prepare their favorite meal.

Bernice Coleman, sister

♥ ♥ ♥ ♥

LESSON 14

Jessie Mae has been such a devoted person in my life. I see her as a sister and not just a sister-in-law because of the bond we have sustained over the years. Jessie Mae has always been there for me and also as a friend. Willie always reached out to help me and my husband, B.C., in any way he could. He has always been a very dependable person to turn to in our time of need and just a good person in general.

Inez Coleman, sister/sister-in-law

♥ ♥ ♥ ♥

The fondest memory I had with Jessie was a conversation about marriage. I don't remember how it started, but I have never forgotten it. She said when there is a marital disagreement, never stop taking care of the other person. You would continue to cook, clean, run errands, etc. Just like nothing happened.

She told me, "Just because you disagree about something, you still love and take care of that person." In essence, I think she was saying that it's okay to agree to disagree. Her wisdom touched me because I was already practicing exactly what she advised, and it made me feel confident in myself.

Cherry Coleman, sister-in-law

♥ ♥ ♥ ♥

I met my husband, W.L., at church. We dated for five years before we got married. When we did marry, Willie came to live with us. He stayed with us for five years until he got married to Jessie. Willie was always so helpful to us. His day off was Wednesday, and he would do all the yard work and the cleaning. The house would be spotless when I got home. The only thing he did not do was cook.

We have always had a close relationship. Willie and W.L. were not only brothers but the best of friends. When they retired, Willie would come over, and they would just sit, talk and laugh for hours. When W.L. passed away, Willie and Jessie always made sure that any time I needed any help, they were there for me. No matter what it is, I know I can depend on them. I know W.L. is proud of how his little brother has helped me over the years since he has been gone. I do not know what I would do without Willie and Jessie.

Minnie Dixon, sister-in-law

♥ ♥ ♥ ♥

My soulmate, Willie L. Dixon, Jr., loved and valued his parents. He always desired their love and acceptance of things he worked so hard for—his wife, daughters, and career in the news media. Jay learned and mastered an amazing work ethic from his parents.

Mom and Dad were also instrumental in helping to form his initial foundation in the Christian faith. Mom and Dad instilled kindness and love of family in his essence. Jay valued and mastered kindness for mankind and enduring love for his family

LESSON 14

while also making a lifetime impact in the media arena. His impact is evidenced by getting a wing of ABC KTRK Channel 13 named after him. I'm forever grateful for your love of Willie L. Dixon, Jr. (my Jay), Dominique, and Sydney.

Dr. Dorothy Brown Dixon, daughter-in-law

♥ ♥ ♥ ♥

Grandma and Granddad have always supported me growing up—even now as an adult. They pour love into me and encourage me to be the best version of myself. We talk often, and they are always interested in how I'm doing and what I am up to. I'm grateful that they are constant positive influences in my life.

Dominique Dixon, granddaughter

♥ ♥ ♥ ♥

My most memorable experience with Willie and Jessie was seeing how much they still love each other. When I first met them, it was like I'd known them all my life. Mama Jessie's famous quote that I love is, "And that's the way that is." My fondest memory of Dad is seeing him ride a bicycle at the age of eighty-three while we were in Anna Maria, Florida, in the summer of August 2021 for a family vacation. He is still just a big kid at heart. Willie and Jessie are prime example of what a marriage should be.

Brent and Felicia Poellnitz, son and daughter-in-law

♥ ♥ ♥ ♥

Wisdom from Willie Jewels from Jessie

Willie and Jessie are some of the sweetest people I know. I have known them for over fifty years. When I moved into our neighborhood, there were mostly white people, so it was nice to have another young black family move nearby.

Willie and Jessie helped me a lot with my son, who also happens to be named Willie. They took him to school every morning in elementary school because I had to go to work so early. I would tell my son to go at a certain time, and he would always go a little earlier because he enjoyed being there so much. Jessie never told me, but she made sure he had breakfast and got to school safely. Willie also helped me around the house when he could. Over the years, we have always gotten along, never having a falling out or disagreement, which is a blessing.

Betty Richardson, neighbor, and friend

♥ ♥ ♥ ♥

Aunt Jessie and Uncle Willie are examples of God's unconditional love and grace. They are the most supportive, truthful, and generous people you'll ever meet. I feel blessed to have them in my life.

Norma Cromwell, niece

♥ ♥ ♥ ♥

LESSON 14

Uncle Willie and Aunt Jessie have always made me feel the love that they had for me. I remember when I was about six years old, I was so scared of Uncle because I thought that he was mean until one day he had to watch me and my brother Curtis while my mom was at work. I realized that day that he was the sweetest man I knew. That's why I always told my mom that Uncle Willie, Aunt Jessie, and Aunt Pecola were my favorite uncle and aunts. I will love them for eternity.

Rhonda Richardson, niece

Jessie is certainly the jewel of our neighborhood. She makes sure everyone is all right, has food to eat, and is comforted in times of sorrow. She always checks on everyone to see how they are doing. When I was diagnosed with breast cancer, she was the first person I told. She talked to me and told me about her family member who had cancer and thrived. She always called to check on me to see how my treatments were going.

When my husband was diagnosed with Covid, I was so tired from helping him. Jessie called and told me she was cooking food for a week, so I would not have to worry about cooking dinner. If anyone's family member passes away in the neighborhood, Jessie is the first one to let everyone know and tell them what she is donating to the family so everyone can support the bereaved family.

There are not many neighborhoods like this anymore. We are more than neighbors; we are family. So, on this street, Jessie is a jewel. One that shines bright for all of us and is there any time we need her.

Willie makes sure we have fresh vegetables, always sharing what he grows in his garden. Like the good book says, love thy neighbor as thyself. Jessie and Willie do just what God says to do, and I am thankful for that.

Charlene and Eugene Phillips, neighbors and friends

♥ ♥ ♥ ♥

I have valued a working relationship with Jessie for over thirty-five years that became a very personal one between my family and the entire Dixon family. Jessie worked for our family as a housekeeper, and in my husband's medical office for many years. We raised children who were the same age and experienced schooling, graduations, marriages, births, illnesses, and, unfortunately, deaths together.

Throughout all that life delivers, I have greatly admired the tenacity, dedication, ingenuity, optimism, faithfulness, and indomitable spirit of both Jessie and Willie. It has been a true privilege to share all these years with two of the loveliest people I've ever known.

Betsy String, employer and friend

♥ ♥ ♥ ♥

LESSON 14

Willie and Jessie Dixon don't meet anyone as a stranger. I can attest to that from how they received me!

Felica Turner, a family friend

♥ ♥ ♥ ♥

Jessie is a God-sent friend, and our friendship has lasted for over forty years. She is a generous person who always gives her time to encourage me when I have problems or just need some advice on making a decision. Jessie also likes to offer contributions and build people up rather than tearing them down in a negative way. Thank you, Jessie, for being a trustworthy and long-life friend to me. I will forever love you and Willie for all the support you've given to my family and me.

Gladys McCants, a family friend

♥ ♥ ♥ ♥

Aunt Jessie has consistently reached out to me, which always makes me feel like a second daughter. She loves and adores her husband, children, and grandchildren. She also purchased my grandchildren seasonal and birthday presents as a selfless expression of kindness.

Uncle Willie is a man of few words but carries tons of wisdom. He will go out of his way to assist anyone he can. One instance he impacted my life was by sharing his knowledge. He saved me $1,200 on automotive repairs by pointing me in the direction of the best mechanics to fix my vehicle. Both Uncle Willie and Aunt Jessie Mae always make you feel welcomed and loved.

Daphne Pettaway, niece

♥ ♥ ♥ ♥

Great-Aunt Jessie has always believed in me. During my college years, I was a nursing student, and although I was doing well, I realized that the nursing profession was not for me. Shortly after becoming a nursing school dropout, I became pregnant with my first son. Great-Aunt Jessie, along with other family members, encouraged me to keep going and never feel sorry for myself. Years later, I graduated in the top fifteen percent of my undergraduate class and the top ten percent of my graduate school class.

Great-Uncle Willie is one of the most thoughtful men I know. I can recall purchasing my first vehicle with my father, and we were uncertain which car had the best engine. My father and I unexpectedly surprised my Uncle Willie at his residence and requested his expert opinion. Great-Uncle Willie popped the hood and gave both engines a rev without thinking twice about the surprise visit. He assisted us in selecting the ideal first car for college. Great-Uncle Willie and Great-Aunt Jessie are truly amazing role models.

Natashia Pettaway, great-niece

♥ ♥ ♥ ♥

LESSON 14

It has been a great pleasure getting to know you two and sharing some fond memories over the past thirty years. Mr. Dixon, thank you for sharing some of your gardening tips with me; they have truly helped me out with my own. I still can't get my tomatoes to grow like yours, but I am still working on it.

Mrs. Dixon, I will continue to say that you are "a mess" from our shared talks that we have had together. You make me laugh constantly, and your amazing memory of years past is a force to be reckoned with.

Thank you both for being awesome adoptive grandparents to my daughters. You are truly loved! One memory that I will always remember of you two is when your son, Jay, took you both to Walt Disney World. We all got on the "It's a Small World" ride, and your smiles lit up from ear to ear. It was priceless!

Terlisa Sheppard, family-in-law

♥ ♥ ♥ ♥

There is so much that I can say about my cousin Jessie. She is a person who cares about another person's feelings and can say the most comforting words of encouragement! She has the ability to share the same feelings that you know you are experiencing in that moment.

My cousin and I have both shared and experienced the loss of a child. Even then, she gave me hope that reminded me that we would see both of them again! I can go on and on about this beautiful, phenomenal woman. I love her very much.

"Carry one another's burdens, and in this way, you will fulfill the law of Christ." (Galatians 6:2 New International Version)

Linda Diane Ridgeway, cousin

♥ ♥ ♥ ♥

I remember every year after Christmas, Aunt Jessie and Uncle Willie would come and visit us in Butler, Alabama. They would bring every family member a Christmas gift. Every fourth of July, my uncles would drive us to Mobile and spend the day with them, and we would partake in the best barbecue on Uncle Willie's grill.

Aunt Jessie Mae bought me a white and black polka dot dress for my senior year to take my senior portrait. She spent countless moments with my mama and her sister Minnie when she came to Mobile for surgery procedures. Aunt Jessie and Uncle Willie always made us feel special and loved.

Shirley Landrum, niece

♥ ♥ ♥ ♥

Aunt Jessie Mae and Uncle Willie have been pillars of the family. They have shown me personally what a marriage should be like and what a husband and father should do. They are examples who show that no matter where you come from, you can be successful in all aspects of life. I love them both. May God continue to bless them.

Terrell Landrum, nephew

♥ ♥ ♥ ♥

LESSON 14

Uncle Willie and Aunt Jessie Mae have a relationship built on strength and love. Aunt Jessie Mae is the matriarch of our family because of her wisdom. I always looked forward to going to Mobile for the fourth of July and Mardi Gras. Aunt Jessie Mae always made our Christmas extra special by bringing us gifts every year.

Uncle Willie and Aunt Jessie Mae are role models for our upcoming generation. They have shown us how to see the best in any situation that arises, and they exemplify what it means to persevere no matter what. I will always be grateful for having them in my life.

Cathy Coleman, niece

♥ ♥ ♥ ♥

Jessie Mae and I have been friends since 1967. She and my ex-husband were high school classmates, which is how we met. Her son Willie Jr. and my daughter Sonia were both born in 1967.

We have had a bond since then because our oldest children attended the same Kindergarten together. We went to Six Flags over Georgia one year on a family vacation, and we have shared our children's and grandchildren's successes throughout the years.

We have never disagreed, nor have we ever had a falling out. She has remained the same over the years, and we still talk on the phone every week. Each time I was hospitalized, she called to check on me, and we had lunch frequently. Now that is a devoted friend. Her husband, Willie Sr., is the same way, and I love them dearly.

Sarah Horne, friend

♥ ♥ ♥ ♥

Thanks for passing down so much wisdom to younger generations. Your words will live forever through all of the lives you've changed and the people you've encouraged. No one will forget their encounters with either of you.

Shantora Hudson, granddaughter-in-law

Willie and Jessie Mae are made for each other. You cannot find a better couple. Jessie Mae and I went to high school together in the ninth grade and graduated the same year. We have been friends ever since. I came to Mobile in 1964, and we maintained our friendship.

I could not have asked for better friends. We have supported each other over the years in both good and bad times. Willie and Jessie Mae are just great people, and I am proud to know them. One thing I will say about Willie, he keeps those cars clean! I wish I could keep mine as clean as he does his.

Levi Horne, friend

♥ ♥ ♥ ♥

Frankie Cornelius, aunt

Inez Coleman, sister-in-law

Betty Richardson, neighbor and friend

Norma Cromwell, niece

Rhonda Richardson, niece

Rev. Eugene and Charlene Phillips, neighbors and friends

Betsy String, employer and friend

Daphne Pettaway, niece

Natashia Pettaway, great-niece

Linda Diane Ridgeway, cousin

Cathy Coleman, niece

Shantora Hudson, granddaughter-in-law

Levi Horne, friend

Sarah Horne, best friend

NOTE: *Some of the contributors to this section are pictured in the book earlier.*

CONCLUSION

By Angela L. Dixon

I hope this book serves as a reminder to you all that your life has meaning. You do not have to have an extravagant life to make a difference to yourself and others. You can be like my parents and live a long and fulfilling life. As long as you are alive, you have valuable contributions to offer to the universe. You can accomplish great things and have a lasting impact because you matter.

Whether you are young, middle-aged, a seasoned senior like Mom and Dad, or anywhere in between, you were made to impact the world. Each person is unique and special, and sometimes, we do not see that in ourselves. Mom and Dad have shared simple lessons that helped them live a long and fulfilling life.

What more will they contribute to this great, big world? I do not know the answer to that question, but I am ready to see and join them as much as I can. I hope their words and stories have encouraged you to take stock of where you are, appreciate your blessed life, and continue to strive to make your life all that it is meant to be. Whether it is to travel, own a home, get married and have a family, save for your future, start a new career or business, give back to your community, or just have fun, it is all within your reach.

We all are in different stages of life, but overall, we all just want to be loved, relevant, understood, and appreciated. We desire to contribute to society and to be lost in the moments of life as they come. Let my mom and dad be an inspiration to the fact that you *can* be fulfilled. You *can* accomplish your dreams and desires, and you *can* enjoy every aspect of life, even when challenges arise. All of this is possible because you were made by a masterful Creator who designed greatness for your life. That greatness may take many forms, but it is up to you to walk in the full power of it. Be blessed, prosper, and *win*!

One final thought: I encourage everyone to explore their family history, talk to their elders and learn about their lives. You may want to write a book, or even if you do not, you can document this information so that it is not lost once the elders are gone. This information can be shared with family members for generations to come. We all have a rich history and amazing stories just waiting to be discovered and shared. Believe me, your life will be enriched more than you can imagine.

♥ ♥ ♥ ♥

ABOUT THE AUTHOR

Angela L. Dixon, Esq., daughter to Willie L. Dixon, Sr., and Jessie M. Dixon, is an attorney, professor, writer, speaker, and mentor. She earned a Bachelor of Arts degree from Alabama A&M University, a Master of Business Administration degree from St. Ambrose University, and a Juris Doctor degree from the University of Iowa College of Law. She has over twenty years of experience as an attorney, handling civil law matters including business, school law, employment law, landlord and tenant, and personal injury law. She also has over fourteen years of experience serving as an adjunct professor, teaching graduate and undergraduate courses for various colleges and universities. She served on the Houston Bar Journal editorial board for several years and rose through the ranks to editor-in-chief.

Angela has been blessed with two of the best parents in the world. They laid a solid and loving foundation, allowing her to become the accomplished person she is today. Having strong and positive values, genuine care and concern for others, giving back, and community involvement all come from being raised in the South by her parents and extended family.

Her wonderful parents, Willie L. Dixon, Sr., eighty-five, and Jessie M. Dixon, seventy-nine, have been married for fifty-seven years. They raised a family and worked for many years to ensure their children could follow and achieve their dreams. They served in their community and have always been dedicated to helping family and friends. They strived to be a positive example and inspiration to others.